THE
LEGAL
JOB
INTERVIEW

The
Legal
Job
Interview

Clifford R. Ennico

BIENNIX CORPORATION
2490 Black Rock Turnpike
Suite 407
Fairfield, Connecticut 06430-2404
U.S.A.

Publisher's Cataloging-in-Publication
(Prepared by Quality Books, Inc.)

Ennico, Clifford Robert, 1954-
    The legal job interview / by Clifford R. Ennico
    p. 182 cm.
    ISBN 0-9632835-5-3

1. Lawyers. 2. Legal assistants.   3. Legal secretaries.
4. Employment interviewing.   I. Title

K116.E5 1992   340.023
                       QBI92-10463

Published by Biennix Corporation, 2490 Black Rock Turnpike, Suite 407,
Fairfield, Connecticut 06430-2404, U.S.A.

Table of Contents

ABOUT THE AUTHOR

To my father, the hero of my childhood

ACKNOWLEDGMENTS

The writing of a book is a solitary job, but getting it into the hands of readers is a team effort. I am very grateful to all of them.

First and foremost, I am indebted to Biennix Corporation for making it possible for me to put my thoughts on paper. Most of the traditional legal publishers are not interested in career guides for lawyers, despite the crying need for them. My hat is off to the entrepreneurial lawyers who formed Biennix precisely to fill this gaping hole in legal literature.

I have dedicated this book to my father, and thank him for his unfailing positive encouragement and support of me; there are times when I felt he was the only one who believed in my crazy dream of becoming a business lawyer and a writer of books the likes of which had never been written before. Without him I would not have grown up sane, much less achieved the dream.

Finally, I could not have written this book without (1) the toleration of my family, out of whose "quality time" all writing projects must come, and (2) the rigorous training-by-fire of the hundreds of lawyers who have interviewed me over the past dozen or so years. Regarding the latter, I hope they are all still employed.

Clifford R. Ennico
Fairfield, Connecticut
June 1, 1992

CHAPTER 1

INTRODUCTION: THE SUBTLE ART
OF BEING INTERVIEWED

A.   *The Changing Legal Job Market*

The young lawyer entering the profession today faces much greater challenges than his counterpart of ten or fifteen years ago. Back then, a lawyer's career path was extremely predictable. He graduated from law school, he passed the bar in a state where he expected to live out the rest of his life, he apprenticed himself to a law firm as an "associate" or salaried employee, and he worked for the firm from five to seven years while developing his skills. At the end of the five to seven year "apprenticeship" period he either was made a partner of the firm (which guaranteed him a job for life) or was "passed over", in which case he easily found a job as partner of a smaller firm in the same town or as "in house" counsel to one of his firm's business clients. Having settled into one of these three positions (partner of the firm where he served his apprenticeship, partner in another firm, or in house counsel to a corporation), he then continued to practice law in his chosen specialty (litigation or courtroom work, corporate law, taxation, real estate, matrimonial, or estates and trusts) until his retirement or death.

Each step in the this career path was very well defined, with very few choices or options. While some lawyers found this narrow track stifling, most found it quite comfortable if not downright cozy. After all, lawyers are not normally inclined, and are certainly not trained, to take risks. The only practical choice for those who could not fit into one of the well established legal career niches was to leave the practice of law entirely, and the list is long of those who have left the legal world for careers in entertainment, politics, government service, business and the arts. Those who stayed in the profession had the luxury of never having to worry about their careers; each step on the treadmill was very well defined, legal employers were careful to "take care of their own", and clients seldom if ever changed lawyers so that once you landed a client (or one was referred to you by a professional colleague) it was pretty much yours for life. The lawyer of bygone days was worried only about keeping his clients happy and staying abreast of developments in the law that affected his practice. Until about a decade ago, a book like this one would have been very short indeed.

The decade of the 1980s saw dramatic changes in the lawyer's traditional career path. Corporations began hiring more lawyers as "in house counsel", in the hopes that by paying them a straight salary instead of an hourly billing rate, they could get a better handle on their spiraling legal costs. Many of these "in house" legal departments have grown to rival in size and competence some of the largest and most prestigious law firms in the United States. During the 1980s, many clients gave up their loyalty to the law firms that had represented them since time immemorial, and spread their legal work among several firms based on the strength of their individual specialties. Clients became increasingly loyal to individual attorneys whose judgment they respected, rather than the firms in which those individual attorneys worked. This shift in client loyalty eventually led savvy lawyers to recognize that if they changed employers their clients would follow.

Finally, during the 1980s law firms became ever more subject to economic pressures, which led them to lay off partners who were not contributing to the firm's bottom line, retire their senior partners early, and fire associates (and partners) in areas of practice that were temporarily or permanently depressed.

The result of these dynamic changes is that the profession of law is no longer a cushy refuge from the realities of the business world. Most lawyers today realize that they cannot count on the traditional career path, much less their current employers, to provide the job security that they were able to do in years past. Today's lawyer must take responsibility for his own career, and "look out for Number One", to an extent that could not be imagined even ten years ago.

Today's lawyer or legal professional (such as a paralegal or law firm administrator) can be expected to change jobs, voluntarily or involuntarily, much more frequently than his counterpart of bygone days. Mobility for lawyers -- from one type of legal environment to another, from one location to another, from one area of practice to another -- is on the rise, leading to greater career insecurity and instability. Lawyers today have to spend a substantial amount of time planning their careers, refining those plans as their career unfolds, keeping their eyes open for changes in the legal environment which may make their current position no longer tenable, and making career transitions. At each stage of their careers, they will spend more time than ever before interviewing for jobs. This book is a guide to the special, and often unique, art of interviewing for a legal job.

B.   The Growing Need For Lawyers To Develop "People Skills", Especially Interviewing Skills

Once upon a time, a lawyer was judged solely on the strength of his technical skills -- his ability to come up with the right answers, win the client's case, get the client's business transaction closed, and provide timely advice to keep the client out of trouble. His ability to deal with people, while never really unimportant, was secondary: a client was quite willing to tolerate a lawyer's eccentricities and idiosyncrasies if he was satisfied with the lawyer's work, and the lawyer's ability to play golf or tennis well could not make up for a failure to understand the client's business and legal problems, or the courtroom procedure necessary to win the client's case.

Today lawyers are inclined to view their work as less of a profession and more of a business. The ability to attract and keep clients, which in earlier times was taken for granted, is today all important. A lawyer who does not have "portable" clients -- clients who view him, and not his firm, as their lawyer and who are willing to follow him from one employer to another -- cannot count on being employed for very long, no matter how much he knows about the law in his field.

The growing pressure on the lawyer to become more attuned to the economics of his practice compel him (in some cases against his will) to develop "people skills" -- the ability to communicate with others outside his profession, the ability to market and "sell himself" to prospective clients, the ability to deal with difficult people, the ability to achieve his objectives through the work of others (which those outside the profession of law call "management"), the ability to win friends and support without being idiosyncratic or "weird" in his behavior, and the ability to convince others that he fits in with them (i.e., that he is "one of them," behaves the same way as they do, and shares their goals and objectives, their ways of getting the job done, their personal style and organizational culture).

Interviewing skills are among the most crucial "people skills" that the young lawyer or legal professional must master in order to be successful in his professional life. Each and every day in the lawyer's life, he is interviewing: eliciting information from his client so that he can analyze the client's problem correctly, persuading a client (or a colleague or a judge) to adopt his point of view and disregard all opposing views, seeking a higher paying or more challenging job, convincing his superiors that he is a more capable lawyer than the person across the hall and therefore more deserving of partnership.

While this book focuses on the skills necessary to survive a legal job interview, the reader should bear in mind that interviewing (in the broadest sense of the word) does not stop when the job offer is made. The wise lawyer who wishes to grow and develop as a professional never stops interviewing, and treats every interpersonal interaction on the job with the same care and caution as if he were in a formal interview situation. Simply put, the successful lawyer or legal professional never "lets his guard down" in a moment of weakness or severe stress; he always conducts himself in such a way as to make the most positive possible impression upon those around him -- he is always in an "interview mode". Wherever an individual desires something from another person over whom he has no control or power, his interviewing skills are the tools that will help him obtain that something.

C.   *A War Story, Or, How I Learned That Legal Interviews Are Different*

When I was seeking my first legal job more than a decade ago, I scoured the business and career sections of every bookstore in town and devoured every book and article I could find on the art of interviewing (even then there were quite a few). I believed at the time that interviewing for a job required a certain amount of acting ability -- I sensed that I could not simply "be myself" in an interview setting, and yet I was not sure exactly how a young lawyer just starting out should present himself. I therefore looked to nonspecialist (i.e. not written for lawyers) books on interviewing for the answers.

I found, however, that even though I was following the rules and principles in these books to the letter, I was not having much success; in some cases it was painfully obvious that I was turning the interviewer right off the minute I opened my mouth. At first I attributed this to my own lack of interviewing skill, which I thought would come in time, or to my own failure to prepare hard enough for the interview, which led me to triple the amount of time spent researching and analyzing prospective employers. All to no avail.

As the rejection letters continued to pile up in a big way, I began to realize that the skills taught in interviewing books were not helping me succeed in my goal of obtaining a legal job, and that a fairly radical change in tactics would be necessary. I slowly began to realize that interviewing for a legal job was much, much different than interviewing for a job in business management, or the media, or government service, or any other occupation on Earth. Sadly, no book had then been written about the special tactics that would be necessary in a legal job interview (to my knowledge, this is the first book on the subject). I could not, of course, rely on words of wisdom I received from other law students; after all, they were my competition. Nor could I rely on advice from legal placement people of my acquaintance, since they themselves had never thought of legal job interviewing in a systematic way and were referring me to the same general interviewing books whose approach I had rejected. Despite excellent credentials, I began to fear that I would never find a first job, much less learn these special tactics for the long run.

I then had an experience which changed my entire life, and taught me in a single, Zen-like flash of intuition what it would take for me to succeed in a legal job interview. I had flown to New York City to interview with several major law firms (I had no difficulty obtaining interviews, so I knew my credentials were not the cause of my troubles). It was the last day before my flight back to law school, and I was scheduled to interview with two firms: I was to spend the morning at Firm A, a freewheeling, intense place known then for its antitrust work, and the afternoon at Firm B, a stuffy, "white shoe" firm that represented many of the old-line investment banking firms on Wall Street.

The morning at Firm A, I thought, went spectacularly well. I met three of the most interesting people I had ever met in my life, and they seemed to love me. We talked animatedly for a couple of hours, and then they invited me to lunch on the spur of the moment (I had not been scheduled for a lunch interview). Three of the firm's top partners took me to a restaurant that was a favorite haunt of movie and television stars, sports figures and Wall Street executives. While there we went through three bottles of wine, and we regaled each other with war stories from our respective pasts (I had been a crime reporter for a daily newspaper before attending law school, and could match them story for story). They wanted me to return to the firm and spend the rest of the day, but I told them I had to catch an early flight because of a Law Review deadline (I couldn't tell them about the interview at Firm B). When we left the restaurant, I thought I was a shoo-in to receive an offer from Firm A.

On the way to my afternoon interview at Firm B, I realized I was not in the best shape for an interview. The wine had made me much too mellow, and I started frantically chewing on breath mints so that this fact would not be too obvious. Even worse, I had gotten so caught up in Firm A's salesmanship that I completely forgot all the information I had gleaned in my extensive research of Firm B. I thought to myself, "Holy Cow, Ennico! You can't go through an interview like this, especially with a stuffy place like Firm B that wants every hair in place. Maybe you should feign illness and ask for a postponement." Then, after a few minutes, I said to myself "hold on a minute. It's going to be weeks before you're back in town again; this may be your last chance for an interview at Firm B. Besides, Firm B is one of Wall Street's most elite law firms; someone with your background probably doesn't have a chance there anyway. You know you've got an offer from Firm A -- you really knocked them dead -- so you don't really need to try so hard with Firm B. Let's just go through the motions at Firm B and get on back to school."

Sure enough, Firm B was as stodgy as I had imagined; the office looked as if it had not been redecorated since the Eisenhower administration. To keep my lack of preparation hidden from view, I sat through a series of interviews with the firm's senior partners in almost total silence. I let them do all the talking (they seemed to like to hear themselves talk). On the rare occasion when they asked me a question or showed any interest at all in me, I thought for a moment, uttered a direct four or five word answer and then countered with a question of my own, which started them off on another tangent for what seemed like hours.

As I left Firm B's offices, I said to myself, "well, you can write that one off. They hardly even seemed interested in you. All they wanted to talk about was themselves and how great they are. They probably took one look at you and said to themselves, 'this guy's not our type.' Frankly, you didn't give them much reason to be interested in you; you just sat there like a bump on a log. Oh well, at least you did well at Firm A; I think you'll be getting an offer from them, so the trip wasn't a total waste."

The letters from Firm A and Firm B arrived the same day. The letter from Firm A was a form rejection letter, just like the dozens of others I'd received. I was crushed. I just couldn't believe I had blown it. I couldn't imagine what I had done wrong. Everything had seemed to go so smoothly, and everyone at Firm A seemed to think I was the greatest thing since sliced bread. I actually (this does not happen to me often) started to cry. Would there be no future for me in the law?

I almost did not open the letter from Firm B. It was in the same sort of envelope as the letter from Firm A, and I had always believed that if you were going to be made an offer it would come in a different size envelope. Besides, hadn't I done a terrible job of interviewing at Firm B? The best I could have hoped to do was hide the fact that I was not prepared for my interview there; those breath mints could not have done the job. I almost threw the unopened letter in the garbage (even today I can't recall what made me open it -- I probably thought that it would complete my collection of rejection letters from New York law firms, which might be worth something to a collector).

The letter from Firm B was not a form letter. It was a personal letter written by the firm's most powerful partner (the autograph alone is probably worth some money today), inviting me to join Firm B as an associate, for a salary so astronomically high that at first I thought it was a typographical error.

I sat on my sofa-bed in stunned silence. What in the world had I done wrong at Firm A, and what in the world had I done right at Firm B? Why were my perceptions of my own performance so off base? Why did I think I had wowed them at Firm A, when in fact I had turned them right off? And why did I think I had made a fool of myself at Firm B, when in fact I gave the best performance of my career? The answer didn't hit me until later that night, after a raucous celebration at the Law Review of my receiving the offer from Firm B.

The reason for my success at Firm B, and my utter failure at Firm A, is the subject of this book. The lessons I learned from that fateful day at Firm A and Firm B are the lessons I teach in this book, so that you won't waste as much time as I did collecting rejection letters from law firms, corporate legal departments, and government agencies.

Once I learned these lessons, I threw away all of the interviewing books I had collected in my job search, because I knew the information contained in them would be utterly

Once I learned these lessons, I threw away all of the interviewing books I had collected in my job search, because I knew the information contained in them would be utterly useless to me in a legal job interview. While I do not suggest that you do the same (they do serve at least two purposes -- providing ready answers to some of the standard interview questions, and showing you how to deal with the "professional interviewer", whom you will undoubtedly encounter at one point or another), I recommend that you take them with a grain of salt. For sometimes these interviewing books are downright harmful to your chances for success. To succeed in a legal job interview, I believe, you must in some cases do exactly the opposite of what other books on interviewing skills will tell you to do. Some of the keys to success in a legal job interview -- which are described in detail in Chapter 4 -- will even seem contrary to common sense, until you apply them in practice and see how well they work.

D.   *What This Book Is All About: Interviewing With Unskilled Interviewers*

This is a very personal book; an essay, not a treatise or textbook. It is not a book of absolute rules, but rather a summary of my own experience in legal job interviews and the lessons I have learned. I have practiced law for more than a decade, in a variety of legal environments, and have made several successful career transitions using the interviewing skills that I have outlined in this book. Still, I cannot hold myself out as an expert on the subject of interviewing. Nor can I guarantee that you will succeed in every legal job interview, even if you follow the lessons in this book scrupulously.

The reason is that there is no such thing as a "typical"

legal job interview.   Personnel and human resources executives in the corporate world are taught how to interview people for jobs, and as a result of this training their approach is somewhat standardized. They do very little of the talking; they ask lots of standard questions, most of which you can anticipate in advance; they ask "negative" questions and sometimes engage in what is called a "stress interview" to see how well you perform under pressure; they are more concerned with "screening you out" than "screening you in"; and so forth.

When you interview for a legal position, on the other hand, your interviewer is not a personnel executive but rather a lawyer just like you (or just like you want to become). Lawyers by definition are not trained in interviewing techniques, as personnel executives are, and so they often don't know the basic rules of interviewing job candidates.

The results can often be amusing, and sometimes can be tragic. In any event they are unpredictable. One of the shortest interviews I ever had was with a large New York City law firm that at the time had the reputation of being a sweatshop. The interviewer said nothing about the firm, and asked only three questions: "are you married?", "what were your billable hours last year?", and "when can you start?" The interviewer made me an offer immediately upon my giving the right answers to these questions ("no," "over 2200 hours," and "as early as next week," in that order), and then left it up to me to figure out whether or not I wanted to work there (I didn't). Those three questions told me more about the firm's attitude toward associates than anything the interviewer actually could have told me.

I recall another interview with a law firm partner whose

office was bedecked with American flags of all sizes and shapes, including one covering an entire wall that looked as if it had flown over the White House at one time. The interviewer asked me questions covering virtually every facet of my personal and professional life, and seemed satisfied with my answers until I made the offhand remark, while answering a question about my summer jobs in college, that "I'm afraid I didn't have too many white collar jobs when I was at college; the summer jobs I did have were more blue collar in nature". The partner scowled, jumped to his feet, banged his fist down hard on his desk, so hard that the flag on the wall became unhinged in one corner, fixed an icy stare at me that made my blood run cold (I thought for a moment he was going to hit me), and shouted through his clenched teeth in a voice I am sure every lawyer in the firm could hear (and that I can still hear to this day), "M-I-S-T-E-R Ennico, the profession of law IS a blue collar job -- in fact, it is the most honorable blue collar job in the United States of America. There is nothing white collar about it. Lawyers are the highest paid factory workers in this country. And don't you ever, ever forget that if you expect to work here, M-I-S-T-E-R Ennico!" Needless to say, I was not too keen on working there either.

You cannot anticipate what the interviewer will do in a legal job interview, the way you can when you are dealing with a professional personnel or human resources executive. So, no amount of planning and preparation will help you win the day. Memorizing dozens of stock answers to stock interview questions could not have helped me in either of the above situations. The trick is to avoid getting into "no win" situations like these with interviewers who obviously haven't a clue how to conduct a successful interview. Instead, your objective is to win the interviewer over by putting him into the position in which he feels most comfortable. Since lawyers are by definition insecure people, who know only too well (in most cases) that they don't have interviewing skills, the best way to win in a legal job interview is to convince the interviewer that he will not need interviewing skills in order to make the right decision about you. As will be seen in Chapter 4, this is a lot easier than it appears at first.

This book is designed to be a complete guide to the legal job interviewing process. Chapter 2 will discuss the legal job interviewer: who he is, how he sees himself, what he is thinking about when you walk into his office (or the placement office at your law school), and what keeps him awake at night when he thinks about his role as interviewer. Chapter 3 will discuss the work you need to do before you schedule a legal job interview. Chapter 4 is the heart of the book, taking you step by step through a typical legal job interview and showing you what to do (and what not to do) to maximize your chances of getting a job offer at a law firm, corporate legal department, or government agency. Chapter 5 discusses some special rules for lunch, cocktail or dinner interviews, whose purpose is often quite different from the in-office interview. Chapter 6, which is not coincidentally the shortest chapter in this book, explains how to negotiate "tangibles" such as salary, benefits, size and type of office, and so forth. Chapter 7 offers some strategies for dealing with the questions you are bound to be asked in a legal job interview, with the caution that you must not follow these formulas too slavishly or else you will appear to be phoney and "programmed" (remember that interviewers may well be reading this book too, and may be on the alert for "Ennico-isms").

Finally, Chapter 8 stresses the need to continue using

your interviewing skills after you have landed the job you want. If this book can be said to have a "conclusion" or a "moral", it is that interviewing skills are the tools of choice whenever you want something from a person (a prospective client, a boss, a member of your personal network, a colleague at another firm) over whom you have no power or control, and that the successful lawyer treats every interpersonal interaction on the job with the same care and caution as he would a legal job interview.

After all, your interviewer's perception of you will be shaped by your performance and demeanor during the job interview. If you act differently after you have been hired, your interviewer will begin to wonder if he made a mistake after all in hiring you, or if he was "taken in" by an acting performance worthy of Sir Laurence Olivier. It is not healthy for your career if your employer thinks that you are something other than what he bought. The purpose of Chapter 8, and this book in general, is to make you aware that interviewing is not merely a job hunting tool, but a career management tool you will employ virtually every day of your professional life.

E.   *Two Short Digressions Before We Begin*

Please keep in mind that this book is about interviewing with lawyers and other nonprofessional interviewers. If you find yourself about to interview with a personnel executive or other professional interviewer -- such as the legal recruitment coordinator of a law firm -- please put this book to one side, and turn instead to one of the many competent books on the subject of interviewing professionally.

Also, you will note that I have decided not to include a chapter on how to interview "when you are a woman or a member of a recognized minority group." While I do not think women and minorities should be unmindful of their status when interviewing for a legal job (there is, sadly, still a good deal of stereotyping and ethnic consciousness in the legal profession), I do not think there really is a "different" way of interviewing when you are a woman or a minority group member. The rules and techniques described in this book should work no matter who you are. Spotting and dealing with discrimination in an interview situation is a topic that is very adequately treated in other books on interviewing, and I did not see the need to discuss it here.

For a different reason, I have chosen to use the masculine pronoun throughout this book, and ask that the reader look upon it as referring to both sexes; in the words of a legal document that once crossed my desk (and which thankfully I did not draft) "the use of the masculine gender in this Agreement shall be deemed to refer to any or all genders or to the neuter gender, as the context may require."

CHAPTER 2

THE LEGAL JOB INTERVIEWER: WHO HE IS, WHAT HE DOES, WHAT HE WANTS TO KNOW

A.   *Knowing Your "Adversary"*

Before you embark on a legal job interview, you must know something about your "adversary" -- the legal interviewer. I have chosen the word "adversary" quite deliberately; the interviewer is not your friend, no matter how warm or enthusiastic he may be during the interview. His role is not to help you find a job, nor is it really to help his employer find the best possible lawyers. He is a gatekeeper, first and foremost: his job is to examine a host of job applicants clamoring at the gate and let pass only those who in his judgment should be given more serious consideration by the organization. As such, he stands between you and your goal -- a legal job -- and if at any time he perceives a conflict between your goal (landing a job with his employer) and his employer's goal (hiring people who are productive and who fit the employer's image), he will always take the side of his employer.

This is not to say you should treat the interviewer in a hostile or adversarial manner -- far from it! It does mean that you should recognize the interviewer for what he is, and be sensitive to his needs, not yours, throughout the interviewing process.

B.   *The Interviewer Is A Lawyer, Not A Professional Interviewer*

This is probably the biggest single difference between the legal job interview and the business job interview. When you interview for a business position, you interview first with a human resources executive -- a professional interviewer who has been extensively trained in the arts of interviewing. Interviewing job candidates is not a peripheral aspect of this individual's job -- it is the very heart of his job, and he is an expert at it. This person will use his considerable skills to screen out those people who do not have the requisite skills for the job or who do not fit the organization's style or "culture". Only after you pass muster with him will you be allowed (along with others) to interview with the people whose decisions really count -- the people in the department or division with whom and for whom you will actually work if you are hired.

By contrast, the legal job interviewing process takes place almost exactly in reverse. Your initial interview will almost always be with a lawyer. What is more, most of the interviews you will go through when seeking a job with a law firm, corporate legal department or government agency will be with lawyers. Only at the tail end of the interview process (often after you have been made an offer to come on board) will you interview with a human resources or personnel executive, whose function at that point often has been reduced to explaining the compensation and benefits package and showing you where the restrooms are.

This simple fact -- that almost all of the interviewers you will face when seeking a legal job are lawyers, not professional interviewers -- is the single most important thing to keep in mind in a legal job interview. If you forget it, and use the techniques described in most interviewing books to try to impress a legal job interviewer, you are likely not to get past first base. Why? Because those interviewing books are written with the professional interviewer -- the trained personnel person -- in mind.

Lawyers view the world much differently than person-nel people; they look for different traits in people than manag-ers do, and value certain skills higher (and lower) than their counterparts in the business world. For example, most lawyers I know detest sales pitches -- anything that smells even re-motely of Madison Avenue "hype" will usually turn a lawyer right off.

If you want to sell to a lawyer, your enthusiasm and dynamic presentation skills will not count for much. What will count is your ability to point out to the lawyer the options available to him and assess -- in a calm, balanced way -- the pros and cons of each option. While you may (and of course should) advocate the course of action you think he should take, you should not "push" it too hard lest you overlook important facts (which the lawyer knows but you may not know) that may dictate another, quite different, course of action. This is after all how the lawyer himself counsels his clients.

The lawyer who is called upon to conduct a legal interview is only too keenly aware how little he knows about interviewing skills. Because lawyers in general are forever insecure about what they do not know (otherwise how do you explain the immense demand for continuing legal education courses?), the interviewer knows he knows nothing about interviewing, and is likely to be quite uncomfortable being in a situation where he knows he lacks the requisite skills. By putting the lawyer-interviewer in a situation where he can survive only by using technical skills that he senses you know better than he does, you will only make him uncomfortable, to your great disadvantage.

The better course is to alleviate the interviewer's anxiety and discomfort by doing as little as possible to show that you consider your meeting with the interviewer as a formal "interview".

In short, success in the legal job interview requires that you carry yourself in such a way that you do not appear to be "interviewing" at all: the lawyer-interviewer will want to have the sort of interaction with you that he knows he will have with you each and every day you are working with him (or for him) on the job. Doing this is not at all easy; some of the specific skills you must master to avoid "coming on too strong" in a legal job interview will be discussed at length in Chapter 4.

C.   *The Interviewer's Job: It Isn't What You Think*

Having established that your interviewer is not a professional when it comes to interviewing job candidates, what exactly is the lawyer-interviewer's job? If you are like most people, before reading this book you would answer that question in one of the following ways: "to find the best candidate for the job", "to screen out the dorks and losers", "to make sure people from XYZ Law School can get in the door at Firm A", or "to make sure Firm A enjoys a favorable reputation with XYZ Law School."

Close, but no cigar. You may think I am being somewhat cynical, but I think the lawyer-interviewer's primary job is
to stay employed with his current employer, and not do anything that will put him at the other end of the legal job interviewing process. His secondary job is to advance to the next
level within his organization: if he is an associate at a law firm,
he wants to make partner; if he is an associate general counsel
of a corporation, he wants to become an assistant general
counsel; and so forth. The plain, simple truth is that success as a
legal job interviewer will not help a lawyer one whit in staying
employed or moving up the legal career ladder; what will count
are his legal skills and his ability to keep clients satisfied, and
the typical lawyer knows that. As a result, there is really no
incentive for the lawyer to become an expert interviewer, and
most lawyers do not take the time or trouble to excel in interviewing.

Even if a lawyer were so inclined, and were willing to
take the time to polish his interviewing skills, he is often too
busy to do so. A lawyer does not cease being a lawyer when
he takes time out from his busy practice to interview legal job
candidates. Often he has to fight to get the time away from his
duties at the office, and even if he is successful he is often
called away from his interview to put out a fire back at the
office. I remember only too well the law firm interviewers
who used to come to my law school; after a long day of back-
to-back interviews, followed by a lengthy dinner at a fancy
restaurant with the most desirable candidates, these poor people
would stagger into the law library and work until all hours of
the morning just to keep up their billable hours and stay current
with their heavy workload.

It should not be too surprising, then, that the lawyer-interviewer is often distracted from the task at hand, or views it as being relatively unimportant. More than any other, the fact that the lawyer-interviewer is a lawyer first and an interviewer second often explains the lawyer-interviewer's behavior during a legal job interview. Because the lawyer does not have the time or the inclination to make in-depth judgments about an individual's talents or qualifications for the job, he is often tempted to "go by the numbers" and pick only those with the most impressive paper credentials, because it is the safest course of action (lawyers always look for the safest course of action) and requires the least risk, analysis and judgment. It also takes the least time, as the lawyer-interviewer cannot bill anyone for his time spent interviewing job candidates (at least ethically he cannot).

D.   The Interviewer's Biggest Concern: Avoiding Mistakes

Because the lawyer-interviewer views interviewing as a peripheral aspect of his work only, he knows that an excellent performance will not get him much recognition by his employer. A poor performance, however, may well make him a laughingstock within his organization. All lawyers wish to avoid the fate of the partner at the prestigious law firm who in the early 1980s hired what appeared to be a highly qualified candidate for a midlevel associate's job, only to discover years later that the candidate had falsified all of her credentials (including her admission to the bar!)

Combine this with the lawyer's natural reluctance to take risks (either for himself or for his clients), and the result is a "cover your rear end at all costs" mentality on the part of the lawyer-interviewer. Simply put, the lawyer-interviewer is most attracted by candidates that will require little selling or explanation within his organization; people whose credentials speak for themselves. That way, if the candidate is hired and fouls something up later on, it is not the lawyer-interviewer's judgment that is at fault, only the candidate's on-the-job performance. If he is hiring law students, he wants a top grade point average and (if possible) Law Review membership; if he is hiring a "lateral" associate from another firm, he wants to see lots of experience doing the precise tasks that are called for in the open position, preferably for a major Wall Street law firm; if he is hiring for a corporate position, he wants to see lots of experience doing the same tasks that are called for in the open position, preferably for a leading company in the same industry; and so forth.

In short, the legal job interviewer is playing a "percentage game" designed to minimize the risk of error; he will not go out of his way to pursue a candidate that he really likes if the candidate's background or credentials will require explanation or defense within the organization. In dealing with the legal job interviewer, you must take pains to appear to fit as closely as possible to the interviewer's mental picture of an ideal candidate for the job, and be realistic in assessing your paper credentials. If you are in the bottom quarter of your law school class and are interviewing for your first legal job, your chances of success are better with the small, local law firms in the area where you grew up than in the large, Wall Street law firm (why? Because your lifelong contacts in the area will help you attract and hold onto clients).

Once you have amassed some experience in private practice and have proven your worth as a lawyer (by winning a big case, let's say, or doing something professionally that attracted lots of local media coverage), you can interview with larger firms with greater confidence, knowing that your law school grades will count for less at that point.

E.   *What The Legal Interviewer Wants To Know*

We have established that the legal job interviewer wants to see candidates that will make his life and his job as easy as possible, and put the hiring decision behind him as quickly as possible so that he may return to his practice and the legal work with which he is more comfortable.

Anticipating what the legal interviewer will want, and giving him what he wants, will depend on the interview situation -- whether you are interviewing for your first job out of law school (or a summer clerkship between the second and third years of law school) or are looking to change jobs or careers after acquiring some experience in the profession.

1.   *For An Entry-Level Position*

You will probably first encounter the lawyer-interviewer in your second year of law school, as you are seeking that all-important summer clerkship between the second and third years. You will certainly encounter him in your third year, as you look for your first permanent position with a law firm, corporate legal department or government agency (this book assumes you are looking for a legal job out of law school; most law students do, although many eventually find their way into nonlegal careers).

What is the interviewer looking for in a law student? The answer will depend on the type of position you are looking for, and where the interview is taking place.

Let's say, for example, that you are looking for a position in a midsized to large law firm in a large metropolitan area. Your run through the legal interviewing process will usually have two steps: an on-campus interview with one or more partners and associates of the firm who have flown into town for the sole purpose of interviewing at your law school; followed (if you successfully get past the first screening) by an all-expenses-paid trip to the firm, where you will be interviewed by a battery of people in their offices and taken out to a restaurant for lunch and/or dinner.

The on-campus interviewers will usually have two traits in common: they are members of their firm's Hiring (or Legal Personnel) Committee, and at least one will be a graduate of your law school. Sometimes the interviewers will bring along one of their junior associates who is a recent graduate of your law school, so that you can see the sort of person they like to hire generally, and so that the interviewers can get the "inside story" on you from that associate. It is not always easy to tell if their primary objective is to find suitable candidates for first-year associate slots at the firm, or to maintain the firm's ties with your law school. Usually it is a little of both.

Sometimes, if you have worked in a particular field or industry before starting law school, you may see the interviewers express some interest in your nonlegal background. This will especially be the case if you worked at one of the firm's corporate clients, or in an industry where the firm has special expertise (a firm that specializes in entertainment law with clients in the music industry may, for example, be very interested in hiring someone who worked as a talent agent and represented some noted musicians; they will not, however, be as interested in someone who spent years pushing buttons in a recording studio, no matter how many autographs he's collected over the years).

Usually, however, this will not be the case, and the interviewers will be interested only in your performance as a law student. The key word here is: credentials. Your grade point average must be high (how high will depend on the firm's reputation; generally, the higher the starting salary for associates, the higher your grade point must be), you should be on the staff of your law school's Law Review or similar publication, and you should have at least some prior connection with the geographic area in which the firm practices (a student who has spent his entire life in New York City and its environs, for example, will have a tough time persuading an interviewer he intends to spend the rest of his life in Kalamazoo, Michigan, unless -- perhaps -- he is engaged or recently married to someone who is a native of Kalamazoo; conversely, it is my experience that New York City law firms never seem to question an individual's willingness to want to come to New York no matter where he is from). Generally, these are the only credentials that really count in an on-campus interview.

Your interest in a specialized field of practice may carry some weight if the firm specializes in that practice and your performance in that specialty is exceptionally high relative to your overall academic performance. For example, if your passion is international law, a firm specializing in international practice may be quite interested in your membership on your law school's Journal of Transnational Legal Studies, your mastery of Mandarin Chinese and Urdu (commonly studied languages like French and Spanish usually don't make the grade here), and the two "books" you earned in international law courses. These focused interests may in fact make up for an otherwise mediocre law school record if the competition has even worse credentials than you do. If, on the other hand, a candidate who is in the top ten percent of his class and a member of Law Review expresses interest in the firm, you will have a difficult time besting him even if his only qualification is that he drives a Japanese car.

I am not saying this is fair, or even good business on the firm's part. It is simply what happens in an on-campus interview. A candidate whose credentials fall below those of the people the firm has hired in the past is someone who needs to be explained or defended within the firm, and few lawyer-interviewers have the time or the willingness to put their career or reputation for good judgment on the line to help someone that, after all, they don't even know.

If your credentials are such that you make it past the on-campus interview, you will usually be invited to spend a day at the firm's offices, where you will interview a number of partners and associates and will be taken to lunch and/or dinner at a fancy restaurant in town. Chapter 5 will describe how you conduct yourself in this situation; our purpose now is to describe briefly what these "on site" interviewers are going to be looking for.

You should first be aware that the individuals with whom you will interview are not selected at random. They are almost always members of the firm's Hiring (or Legal Personnel) Committee; sometimes a firm will not put you to a vote until you have been seen by all of the Committee's members. Most will be partners, although some associates will usually be thrown in for good measure. If you have expressed interest in a particular area of the firm's practice, you may also interview with one or two partners in that area who are not members of the Committee. Finally, you may spend some time talking to an important nonlawyer -- the staff person who coordinates the firm's law school recruiting effort; usually she (for some reason it is almost always a female) or one of her assistants will walk you from one interview to the next and keep you on your schedule.

What are these "on site" lawyer-interviewers looking for? Let's start with the partners. While your credentials are still important at this stage, and you may be certain you will have to repeat much of the information you doled out at the on-campus interview, what is even more important is your perceived "fit" with the firm's style, culture and personnel.

As you walk through the hallowed hallways of Firm A or Corporation B, your interviewers will be looking around and asking themselves, "does he go with the furniture?" Are they comfortable dealing with you? Do you carry yourself the same way others in the firm do (note that this is different from asking "do you carry yourself well generally")? Is your image a professional one? Do you appear to be diligent and hard-working? Do you appear to have good judgment? Are you "one of us"? Do you dress, walk, eat like we do? Will our clients like you?

As you can see, these are extremely subjective questions; no two individuals are likely to come up with precisely the same answer. Moreover, it is not likely that any of your interviewers will ask these questions outright; indeed, an employer could get into a fair amount of legal trouble if their interviewers did so. Sometimes, however, it does happen: I recall vividly that once when I was looking for a summer clerkship at my law school I interviewed with a partner of a prominent firm in a fairly large city in the Deep South. He listened intently to my expression of interest in the firm's work (which was genuine -- the firm had a unique specialty that I was interested in at the time), but a quizzical look in his eye told me he wasn't completely convinced. Finally, he leaned over and said in a thick Southern drawl "Mister Inn-EEE-ko, let me ask you something point blank. Most of our clients here are what you might call hillbilly rednecks -- Good Old Boys who have a little too much to drink on a Saturday night, say the wrong things to the wrong people, and get themselves thrown in jail. You've spent your entire life up North. Do you really think you would be comfortable dealing with clients like that?" The real question, of course, which he probably did not think it proper to ask, was "would our clientele be comfortable baring their souls to someone whose background is so different from theirs?"

Whether a person's cultural "fit" with an employer is a legitimate criterion for employment is a question much debated in legal circles these days, and is beyond the scope of this book. Yet as a general rule I believe that the farther along you go in interviewing with a particular legal employer, the less important your paper credentials become, and the more important these intangible questions of "fitting in" become. You must adjust your interviewing style accordingly; whatever you actually say during each "on site" interview, you must convince each interviewer that you were born to work for that firm. The fact that your Law Review case comment is going to be published may well be less important to the interviewer than the fact that you wear plaid sport jackets when the firm "look" is pin-striped suits.

I have never personally sat in on a Legal Personnel Committee meeting of a law firm where candidates are being discussed. I have heard, however, and I personally believe, that decisions are made more by consensus than by majority vote. In order to succeed in the "on-site" interview you have to impress favorably almost all of the people who interview you. The one you turn off may well be Chairperson of the Committee, unbeknownst to you.

Before we leave the "on site" interview, a few words about those associates on the Committee and the nonlawyer staff person who walks you around from interview to interview. It is very tempting in an "on site" interview to save your best performances for the partners you are meeting, and "relax" a bit more when talking to the associates. I believe this is a tragic mistake. The associates who sit on the firm's Legal Personnel Committee are a special breed; usually they are hand-picked by the partners on the Committee, who are often among the most powerful partners in the firm. Indeed, one of the best ways to identify the up-and-coming associates in a large law firm is to see which ones are named to sit on the Legal Personnel Committee; some of them may indeed think they are already partners. This tells you right away that their primary loyalty is not to you, the candidate.

While they will sit in on the Committee meeting that determines whether or not you will be made a job offer, and may well have a vote, you can bet that their favorable opinions of you will not be as important to your future as those of the partners on the Committee. They do, however, serve a very important function: to obtain information about you that would not come out in a partner-level interview, where you supposedly are on your "best behavior". Sometimes they will go out of their way to get you to "relax" and reveal information that will tell the partners you really are not "one of them". Watch out especially if you are taken to lunch by a group of associates with no partners present; being away from the office may tempt you to "tell tales out of school". Be assured these associates are smart enough never to do that. Remember Firm A from Chapter 1, that took me to lunch at the steak house frequented by movie stars and corporate moguls? There wasn't a partner in the group.

The same rule applies to the nonlawyer who walks you around the office; there is a strong temptation either to talk to her as if she is unimportant (because she is a nonlawyer), or to "open up" when talking to her in the mistaken belief that the lawyers on the Committee don't listen to her. This latter temptation is especially great, because you're much more likely to let your guard down while walking through the hallways than when sitting in someone's office.

The nonlawyer is quite likely to sit in on the Committee's evaluation meeting, and if her view of you is markedly different from the lawyers' view, she will be listened to. In some firms, she may be charged with the task of determining how you will interact with the firm's nonlawyer staff (secretaries, messengers, librarians and so forth); if she perceives that you are likely to be cruel to staff people (because you treated her as if she didn't exist) or act improperly toward them (because you tried to pick her up), it may be the kiss of death to your candidacy at that firm.

Up to now we have been talking about firms that follow a two-step approach in interviewing law students: an "on campus" interview followed by a series of "on site" interviews.

Of course, the law firms who choose to follow this route tend to be the biggest and most prestigious, with the resources to fly their lawyers around the country interviewing on law school campuses, fly candidates from distant locations to interview at the firm, and pay the candidates' hotel bills. They constitute only a very small percentage of the total number of legal employers, and they certainly have no monopoly on good quality legal work.

Most law students, in fact, will not find their first jobs in this fashion. Rather, they will identify one or more geographic locations in which they want to work, and focus their attention on the small to medium sized law firms in each location. They will send to each firm a copy of their resume and a short cover letter, stating that "I plan to be in your city the week of XXX, and will call you in the next few days to see if you would have some time to meet with me during my stay." They then will schedule a block of interviews in their target location, and will usually pay their own airfare and hotel bills (most often, since the target location is the place where they grew up, they will stay with their parents or other relatives). Thus there will be no "on campus" interview.

Generally, a small to medium sized firm that is approached in this fashion will be less concerned about the candidate's credentials, although this cannot be presumed in all cases. If you look through the Martindale-Hubbell Legal Directory and its description of the small to medium sized firms in a particular area, you will note that the vast majority of lawyers in those firms graduated from law schools in that area. If you are graduating from a law school outside of that area (unless of course it is one of the prestigious, highly visible national law schools), your credentials may have to be as good as if you are interviewing at a large law firm.

What will be more important to a small to medium sized firm are (1) the candidate's commitment to work in that geographical location, (2) the candidate's commitment to doing the particular type of work that that firm does (unlike a large law firm, the smaller law firm cannot usually give the candidate a choice of work; if the firm does mostly wills and divorces, you will have to enjoy doing wills and divorces), and (3) the candidate's potential for keeping the firm's existing clients satisfied and bringing in new clients (unlike a large law firm, there usually will be no room for the candidate to make partner unless he builds a client base of his own).

This does not mean that questions of "fit" are irrelevant in the smaller firm environment. Far from it! A small to medium sized law firm is like a family; the partners and associates tend to be more supportive of each other, just as in a family, but just like a family there can be a certain tendency to "smother" the individual, and there will usually be a strong sense of firm identity. Both you and the firm will be extremely unhappy if you are not totally committed to the "family business". As one partner of a very small firm once explained to me, "in a place like this it's very important that people see you are on the bus, going the same place that we are; if people have to worry about whether or not you're on the bus, that's going to be a big problem." Ironically, this is not as much a concern in the larger law firm, where there is an expectation that many if not most of the young associates hired each year will eventually leave for greener pastures. The question of "fit" is, however, looked at differently in the smaller firm. In the large firm, the question is "does the candidate fit the firm's image" or "does he look right?" In a smaller firm, the question is more likely to be phrased "does the candidate have what it takes to be a productive member of the family" or "is he going to be able to hack it for the long term?"

2. *For A "Lateral Hire" Or Career Change*

First, let's define some key terms. By a "lateral hire", I mean a job change made after one has been practicing law for a while, in which one is looking for a job in a different legal environment -- for example, from a large law firm to a smaller law firm, from a law firm in City A to a law firm in City B, or from a law firm to a corporate legal department or government agency (or vice versa).

Where one is looking to change the focus of one's practice -- from a general corporate practice to bankruptcy work, for example -- I call it a "career change."

Obviously, one may be looking to make a lateral move and a career change at the same time; I would argue, however, that changing both one's practice and one's legal environment at the same time is an extremely difficult move. Once you have started in practice and developed a track record in one or more legal specialties (no matter how short), you tend to become a "prisoner of your resume"; people looking at your track record will assume that you did something in your life because you enjoyed doing it, and that you want to avoid making radical breaks with your past. Simply put, the longer you stay in the profession, the harder it is to make jagged, radical changes in your career path. You will find, I think, that most people who have made radical changes in their careers have done so only gradually and incrementally: they moved from a larger to a smaller firm first, for example, and then slowly began building up experience in a new and different area of practice as their colleagues gave them "overspill" work to do in that area.

You will most likely find that at this point in your career your experience will count for more than your academic credentials; you are not likely to be grilled about your grade point average, and you should be slightly insulted if your interviewer asks to see a law school transcript after you have been out of school more than a couple of years (if you are looking for another position within your first two to three years of practice, however, your academics may still be important, as you have not had enough time to build up a track record). Your academic record may, however, help support your argument for a career change ("I've enjoyed my two years of corporate work, Ms. Jones, but looking back over my academic record I can't help noticing that my best grades were in procedure-related courses and moot courts; I really loved those courses, and my gut tells me that I would be a better fit in litigation").

One of the questions you are bound to be asked during a job interview will be: "why do you want to make a change at this point?" (or "what do you see in us that you don't see in your current employer?"). We will deal with this question in Chapter 7, and suggest a strategy for providing the "right" answer. The important point now is that this question has only two possible answers (or some combination of the two): you must be convinced (and be able to convince your interviewer) either that you are better suited to a different type of work that is not done at your current employer (or that is done much better at your prospective new employer), or that your "fit" with another employer will be better than it is at your current employer. The first approach identifies you as a career changer, the second tells the interviewer you are in a "lateral" situation.

The lawyer-interviewer's concerns with a "lateral hire" or "career change" candidate will often mirror the candidate's own concerns. When looking at such a candidate, the lawyer-interviewer wants to know the answers to three questions: "does this candidate have skills and/or contacts that we need here right now?", "would this candidate fit in better here than with his current employer?" and "is this candidate a threat to my job security?" The answer to the first two questions must be "yes", to the third "no." Let's look at each of these questions in turn.

First, "does this candidate have skills and/or contacts that we need here right now?" When you are interviewing for a position right out of law school, interviewers usually are not too concerned about your chosen field of practice (although they may ask about your interests). They know that you yourself probably don't have a good idea what you want to do; that's why most of the larger law firms have "rotations" in the first couple of years, where you are given the opportunity to sample a variety of legal specialties with (sometimes) some choice over your future direction within the firm. In a smaller law firm, of course, these options do not exist: the interviewer will not ask what you want to do, but will rather tell you what the firm does, and you will have to enjoy doing what the firm does because they don't have any choice over their workload themselves.

It is different when you are in the "lateral hiring" or "career changing" mode. A law firm, corporate legal department or government agency often does not have the time, and cannot afford, to train people in new areas or fields of practice. If they are in the market for a "lateral hire", they usually will want someone who can "hit the ground running" and begin contributing to the bottom line from his first day of employment. The skills that you have learned with your current employer, the substantive areas of law you have mastered, and the types of transactions you can do in your sleep, are the sorts of things the lawyer-interviewer will want to know a great deal about.

Rarely will you have all of the skills needed to survive in a lateral position, but you must have at least some carryover skills for which your prospective new employer has an immediate need. As for the rest (the skills you have not yet learned, the transactions you still must master), you must convince the interviewer that you have had at least some exposure to them and have a proven track record as a "quick study" that will enable you to climb up your learning curve quickly.

In the "career changing" situation, the interviewer will be asking himself the following questions: "what sort of experience has the candidate had that makes him think he's better at corporate work than litigation?", "do we have sufficient corporate work that we can afford to train someone at his level?", "is the candidate more likely to succeed in corporate work than in litigation?", and "is this candidate sufficiently convinced that corporate practice is his true life's work, or will he change his mind later on (and head off somewhere else) after he finds out how dull it is?"

The career changer will usually find success only in one of two situations: either the employer is so desperate for people in a certain area that it is willing to train the new employee who has only marginal contact with that area of practice, or the employer will insist that the candidate start working in the new area at a reduced salary and a more junior level than the candidate enjoys at his current employer (for example, if you are a fourth-year associate at your current employer, the interviewer may say, "we're interested in bringing on more bankruptcy lawyers, but not at your level; if you want to pursue this change in practice, you will have to consider coming on board as a second-year associate").

Second, the lawyer-interviewer looking at a "lateral hire" or career changer will want to know, "would this candidate fit in better here than with his current employer?" The question of "fit" is an all-important one in the "lateral hiring" situation, both for the candidate and the lawyer-interviewer. After all, the candidate is seeking to do the same sort of work that he is presently doing, so that alone cannot explain the change. The candidate must convince the lawyer-interviewer that he seeks a higher quality practice, a practice located closer to home, a slightly different focus to his practice (for example, a bankruptcy lawyer who has represented mostly corporations and business entities may want to expand his experience in handling individual bankruptcies), a chance to build his own clientele, practice in a different environment, or some other plausible reason for changing jobs that does not signal a desire to change careers.

I do not believe it is wise for a candidate to try a "lateral move" and a "career change" at the same time. The candidate must wrestle with his conscience and ask the hard question "what is it about my current situation that I really detest?" If the answer comes back, "the work I am doing", the candidate will have a much easier time moving into a similar legal environment where he can do the work he enjoys doing and then, after a couple of years, move into a different legal environment if he so desires. Similarly, if the answer comes back, "the environment I am in" (for example, the candidate hates working the long hours that are requiring in a large law firm), he is better advised to change his environment first and then seek work in areas of practice that are more to his liking (in a smaller law firm, for example, the hours are usually more flexible, and the candidate will have to learn new areas of practice as few small law firms can afford the luxury of specialization).

Finally, the lawyer-interviewer looking at a "lateral hire" or "career change" candidate will ask himself: "will this candidate threaten my job security?" By definition, newly minted lawyers fresh out of law school are not threatening to their superiors: they know nothing, and usually are quite aware that they know nothing, about the practice of law, and are looking to gain experience and "get their feet wet" more than they are looking to climb the career ladder. An overwhelming majority of these new lawyers will leave their jobs within the first five years of practice and move on elsewhere, and the more senior lawyers within the organization know that.

The same cannot be said of the "lateral hire" or the career changer, who has some idea of what he wants out of his work and wants to be viewed as a contender for success in his chosen field. The lawyer-interviewer will usually occupy a higher rung on the same ladder the candidate wants to climb, and will want to be sure he is not bringing on board the "Young Turk" that will knock him off that ladder.

A candidate who convinces the lawyer-interviewer that he has extremely strong skills in his field and a terrific potential for expanding the employer's client base in a dramatic way, may be doing himself as much harm as good because he will scare the living daylights out of the interviewer (keep in mind that most lawyers are insecure by nature, and constantly question their abilities, their talents and their success -- paradoxitfor cally, it is this natural insecurity that makes them successful; because of it successful lawyers overlook no detail, however small, and take no risks, however small). After all, the interviewer is the "gatekeeper" that determines who comes into the organization, and who stays out; while his support of a candidate may be subject to some scrutiny by others within the organization, his decision to keep someone out almost certainly will not be questioned ("I just didn't think he would fit in here; much too aggressive", and so forth).

If this sounds unfair to you, you should put yourself for a moment into the interviewer's shoes. If you were insecure about your talents and skills in your current job, and you were worried about being able to hold onto that job over the long erm, what thoughts would be going through your mind when interviewing the "perfect" candidate for a job that could well lead to your position in a couple of years (or a few months)? Would you say to yourself, "his credentials are perfect; I will be doing a great service to my career by sponsoring him and giving him a chance to take over my job in a year or so." Of course you wouldn't! You would much rather be talking to someone whom you could "mentor" -- someone who knows even less about the field than you do, with a personality that is nonaggressive, self-effacing and unchallenging.

You may be saying to yourself, "wait a minute, Mr. Ennico! What you are suggesting is that employers do not seek the best candidates for a position, but often are actually looking mediocrities that won't be a threat to them; how can we compete with the Japanese if we do that?" A good question indeed. The Japanese get around this, of course, by the rigid seniority system in most Japanese organizations: if you are an employee of a Japanese corporation, for example, and you are thirty years old, you simply will never be in a position to challenge the authority or leadership of someone in that organization who is thirty-five or forty years old. It just isn't done; you are expected to wait your turn. So senior Japanese executives do not worry as much as their American counterparts do about the inadvertent hiring of their replacements.

I do not advocate that we adopt the Japanese management system in this country; I merely point out that there is good news and bad news in the American style of management. The good news is that you can indeed unseat someone many years your senior if you have the superior talent, aggressiveness, judgment and poliical survival skills to do so.

This is, by the way, what is meant in most organizations by "team playership". Very often the people who make it to the top in organizations, or who survive the inevitable downsizings and cutbacks, are people who at first blush are not very impressive. Sometimes they appear to be wimps with little talent, and people will wonder "how did someone like Charlie ever become Vice President?" I suggest to you that these people are in fact quite impressive, and deserving of their succes, because they have learned the difficult lessons of political survival better than their "smarter" and "more qualified" competitors.

"Coming on too strong" in a legal job interview is one of the cardinal sins that we will discuss at length in Chapter 4.

CHAPTER 3

BEFORE THE LEGAL JOB INTERVIEW

A.   *The Importance of Knowing What You Want*

Success in a legal job interview, as in any other professional endeavor, requires preparation and thought. There
should be no surprises during the interview itself: you should
know what you want, you should anticipate what the lawyer-
interviewer wants, you should have ready answers to the
standard interview questions, you should have in your mind a
list of questions to fill awkward silences, and (most important of
all) you should want the job.

No one should ever waste time interviewing for a job
they know they will not like; even if they are successful in
getting an offer, they will be in a double bind. If they reject the
offer, they demonstrate bad faith to the prospective employer,
which can only hurt them in the long run (legal employers have
long memories, and the legal community, while large, is still
small enough that you are certain to encounter some of these
people in your practice later on). If they accept the offer, they
are committed to a job in which the odds for success are re-
mote, and the odds of failure high. Why? Because in the long
run no one can succeed doing work that they don't like doing,
or being in a job that they know is a dead end for them.

I repeat: you should never walk into an interview
situation without knowing in advance that the position, if
offered to you, is one you would accept. You will not have this
knowledge without doing your homework, sizing up the potential employer, and sizing up the people who are most likely to

be your lawyer-interviewers. This chapter discusses the things you should do before you walk into the interview room.

B.   Doing Your Homework

It is elementary that before interviewing with a particular employer, you must know something about that employer. If the prospective employer is a law firm, you must know how large (or small) the firm, the backgrounds of the key partners, who the key clients are (and how strongly they are attached to the firm), the areas of practice in which the firm specializes, which of these specialties are strong, which are weak, and so forth.

If the prospective employer is a corporation, you must know each of its lines of business, the industry (or industries) in which it competes, the outlook and prospects for each line of business, the financial health of the company as reflected in annual reports and filings with the Securities and Exchange Commission (if its stock is publicly traded), its brands and trademarks, and so forth.

If the prospective employer is a government agency, you must know its mission as set forth in federal or state statutes, the programs which it administers, the tasks lawyers are called upon to play within the agency (in the Department of Justice or a prosecutor's office, it is likely to be litigation, in the Securities and Exchange Commission or a state "blue sky" office it is likely to be document review), the agency's reputation, and so forth.

1.   *Traditional Ways of Researching Employers*

What are the traditional ways of finding out this information? In days gone by, the untutored would (1) look up the employer in the Martindale-Hubbell Legal Directory or the Prentice-Hall Directory of Corporate Counsel; (2) read the firm resume in his law school's placement office (or obtain a copy from the firm's legal recruitment coordinator), keeping in mind that it is intended as a marketing tool, not an objective statistical description of the firm; and (3) if the employer is a corporation, look at the annual report and the latest annual filing with the Securities and Exchange Commission (if the company's stock is publicly traded).

While I do not belittle the necessity of doing this type of exhaustive "library research" (indeed there is a wealth of information in these volumes, if you are thorough and patient), I do feel it necessary to point out some major limitations of this method of preparing for a legal job interview.

2.   *The Problem of Time Management*

First, doing this sort of research takes time, and lawyers (including law students) have little if any time for nonessential activities. If you are a law student, there are classes to attend, examinations to study for, papers to write, and Law Review work to be done. If you are a practicing lawyer, there are hours to bill, briefs and memoranda to write, documents to draft, and meetings to attend. I have learned that the more things you plan to do to prepare adequately for a job interview, the less likely you are to do any of them, with predictable results. Indeed, I doubt that most candidates for legal jobs manage to spend more than a few minutes looking at the employer's Martindale Hubbell entry before walking into the interview room.

3.   *Weaknesses of the Traditional Research Materials*

Second, even if you do find the time for careful research, I question the value of the information you are likely to get from the traditional sources. Your research is wasted activity unless it is focused on helping you do two things: determine whether you would want to work for a particular employer, and help you formulate intelligent questions to ask the lawyer-interviewer for that employer. The statistical information you will be able to glean from Martindale-Hubbell, the firm resume or the corporation's annual report is not designed to disclose the "inside info" you need to be able to answer these two questions satisfactorily.

Sometimes the traditional sources, aside from being merely useless, can be grossly misleading and lead you down a disastrous career path. Anyone reading the 1986 Martindale-Hubbell entry for the New York law firm of Finley, Kumble, Wagner, Underberg, Manley, Myerson & Casey would think it one of the most solid, reputable, indestructible firms in America. The entry contains page after page of impressive biographies, seemingly without end. As is well known, the firm filed for bankruptcy protection in early 1990 and subsequently dissolved amid charges that partners grossly mismanaged the firm; the courts are still trying to clean up the mess.

Even if the information you obtain from these traditional sources is reliable, statistical-type information just isn't very helpful when you are trying to sell yourself to an interviewer. Few lawyer-interviewers I know are likely to be impressed by your knowing that the firm has 150 lawyers with offices in five states (including Washington D.C.), specializes in commodities litigation, and just recently won a major case before the United States Supreme Court on the rights of commodities brokers to require arbitration of customer claims. Either they assume you already know this (a lawyer-interviewer will never quiz you on your knowledge of the employer's business), or they will think you are trying to "show off". In any event, by spouting off this type of information you are not telling them anything that they don't already know; after all, they wrote the firm resume and told Martindale-Hubbell what to say about them.

The type of information you will need to know in order to determine whether you are interested in a particular employer, and impress a lawyer-interviewer from that employer, is likely to come from sources other than the traditional ones. You should take the time to explore these nontraditional routes. Fortunately, access to this information is not expensive or time-consuming, and requires only that you make a couple of telephone calls, keep your eyes open at a couple of critical moments, and spend not more than a few minutes per interview doing some basic research in the law library.

C.   *Sizing Up The Potential Employer*

1.   *Happiness Is a Good "Fit"*

We have established that statistical information can sometimes be misleading, and will almost never give you a living, breathing portrait of your prospective employer in action. Ultimately, whether or not you will be happy in a given work environment will depend not on the size of the firm, or the net earnings of the company over the last five years, or the fact that a majority of the firm's partners graduated from the same law school as you did, but rather will depend on how closely you fit with the employer's style and culture, and how well you like working with the people you will find there. Without belittling Martindale-Hubbell or Fortune magazine's listing of the top 500 corporations in America, there is no way for you to learn this important yet intangible information from a directory or other traditional research source.

2.   *The Two Cardinal Rules of Job Research*

In my experience, there are two cardinal rules when researching a potential employer: (1) gossip or "soft" information is much more important than statistical or "hard" information; and (2) what you see or hear leaves a more lasting impression in your mind, and is therefore more easily remembered, than what you read or write. Let's look at each of these rules and see how they apply to researching legal job opportunities.

a.   The Importance of "Gossip"

Why is gossip so important? Because unfortunately, there is not yet published a definitive "guide to corporate cultures" that can help you determine how political or "cutthroat" a work environment is, the rate of employee turnover, the number of reductions in force or "downsizings" that have occurred over the past couple of years, whether the hours are naturally or artificially long (in the legal profession they will almost never be short, unless you seek a part-time position), whether there is an emphasis on a particular ethnic group or practice area within the employer, the extent to which junior lawyers are given responsibility for handling matters and dealing with clients, and so forth.

Sadly, as in many other areas of life, there is a tradeoff in researching a potential employer: obtaining the more intangible or "touchy feely" information about an employer involves accepting a lower standard of reliabiity than will be the case with "hard", statistical information about that employer. This is because much of this intangible information is subjective; one person's sweatshop is another's paradise, and one person's "cutthroat" environment is another's "dynamic, aggressive" culture. More importantly, much intangible information about an employer will tend to come from people who are at some remove from the employer: former employees whose information may not be up-to-date; people who know the employer only by reputation or by casual contact (for example, the attorney at another firm who has argued or negotiated against attorneys at the firm you want to know about); journalists who have written magazine articles about the employer, often without having any formal training in business or law or experience in the employer's industry; information compiled by trade associations or journals; and the like.

The best, and most reliable, source of intangible information about an employer are, of course, people like yourself who work there in the position for which you are interviewing. These sources must be handled with care, and the information they provide "weighted" to account for their position within the organization. A senior associate at a large law firm who is up for partnership this year, for example, is "walking on egg-shells" and is not likely to say anything bad about his employer for fear it will get back to the powers on the Legal Personnel Committee. A first-year associate at the same firm may not be as committed to the firm but also does not have the experience to see the "big picture". Because you do not know who talks to whom within the employer, you would not want to ask any question you would not ask an interviewer from that employer; this will further reduce the value of the information you obtain.

This is not to say that you should not contact people at the target employer (although of course you should do so as discreetly as possible), only that you will seldom be able to get the best information out of them in a way that will not increase the risk of your being "screened out" of the interview process. For the same reason that I never read a biography of a politician who is still in office (he's not about to write about the "good stuff" because he still needs to remain on good terms with a lot of people), but only a politician who has retired (and is therefore free to "tell all" within the limits of the libel laws), I believe that the best source of intangible information about an employer (although certainly not the most unbiased) is someone who has recently left that employer under generally favorable conditions.

b.   *Don't Read; Watch and Listen*

The second cardinal rule of researching a potential employer is that "what you see or hear leaves a more lasting impression in your mind, and therefore is more easily remembered, that what you read or write." I do not have a background in cognitive psychology, but I find I have an easier time remembering "war stories" and cases, especially if they were particularly vivid or funny, than I do Law Review articles, hornbook chapters, or legal outlines. I believe the same is true in researching a potential employer.

Once I was looking at a career opportunity at a smaller law firm (let's call it "Firm Y"). I met with Firm Y's "name partner", and found him an awfully sweet and likable person; some of the other attorneys looked a bit haggard around the edges, but I attributed this to the nature of the practice. Several days later I met with another lawyer in the same community, who without any prodding from me volunteered that Firm Y was a notorious sweatshop whose name partner "while he always comes across as a sweet and likable person, has a reputation for taking you for everything you're worth once your foot is in the door; unless you get an employment agreement in writing with him, you'll end up working 90 hours a week for a salary that won't even pay your rent." Without suggesting that I was talking to Firm Y, I called up three other lawyers in the same community, all of whom confirmed Firm Y's reputation as a sweatshop and the name partner's trickiness in dealing with new hires. While this of course was only circumstantial evidence, there is an old saying that "if one person calls me a horse, I laugh; if three people call me a horse, I go out and buy a saddle." I did not pursue the opportunity at Firm Y any further.

3.   *So How SHOULD You Research An Employer?*

How should you research a potential employer? Keeping in mind the two cardinal rules of researching a potential employer, I would suggest that you focus first on magazine and journal articles about the employer, and then try to network through to someone who can give you the inside information you really need, either in person or over the telephone. Moreover, you should spend about 25% of your available research time on the first task, and 75% on the second: a good personal contact will always be ten times more useful than a written source.

a.   *Magazine Articles: The More Gossip, The Better*

You should begin with articles about the employer that have appeared in business magazines and trade journals. You can look these up in the *Reader's Guide to Periodical Literature* and the *Index to Business Periodicals* available at any library. With respect to law firms, which often are not written about in the business press, you should go to a law library (usually there will be one in or near your county courthouse or at a local law school which will give nonstudents limited access) and look up the employer's name in the index to theNational Law Journal, The American Lawyer or any other regional or local publication that focuses on the legal profession, not developments in the law itself (a state bar journal or the American Bar Association's magazines, for example, will not have the type of information you need). When reading magazine articles, especially those in general business magazines such as Fortune, Forbes and Business Week, try to stay clear of articles on a specific new development (for example, the employer's introduction of a new product, or the appointment of a new chief executive officer). Try instead to find articles describing general trends in the employer's industry, business lines or financial condition. Usually you can tell from the headline, which is usually re-printed in the standard indices, whether the article is specific or general in nature.

Keep in mind that magazine articles are fine, but they represent the view of an outsider looking in, not an insider (as you want to be) looking out. Reporters after all are only as good as their sources, and lawyers are notoriously reticent to tell outsiders what really goes on at their shops (something to do with preserving client confidentiality and all that). More-over, journalists value their sources, and usually will not di-vulge information if the risk of losing a valued source out-weighs the newsworthiness of the information.

Generally, given the choice, I play down articles in general business magazines, and focus my attention instead on articles in industry trade journals. While these are subject to some of the same restrictions as general business magazines (the need to avoid offending sources, for example), they tend to be written by people who are more experienced with the industry and the key "players" in that industry, and so tend to ask the right questions more frequently. If you are lucky enough that your prospective employer is in an industry with a highly respected newsletter which also publishes industry gossip (such as Asset Sales Report, a biweekly publication that reports on developments in the structured finance industry on Wall Street), you should know what that newsletter has written about your target employer, and may even want to call one of the editors for some "behind the scenes" information (if the publication is small enough, the editors may be extremely flattered that you thought enough of them to call, and will usually be co-operative if they think you will eventually become a subscriber -- or better yet a source of industry information once you find employment).

b.   How to Read The Employer's Own Literature

While magazine and trade journal articles are good sources of the "right" information about an employer, they are only the starting points of your research. If you are interviewing with a law firm or corporation, you should at least glance at the firm resume or the corporation's annual report, but not for any hard, statistical information that may be printed there. Look instead for clues to the organization's structure and future plans. In an annual report, for example, I would read the president's message to shareholders. How optimistic or pessimistic is senior management about the company's future? Which lines of business have performed, and which have not (you don't want to be hired by a poorly performing unit -- they are the first to downsize)?

You should read also the brief descriptions of the corporation's business lines. Which are the core businesses, and which lie at the periphery (the latter will be the first to be sold off or shut down)? In the corporation's proxy statement and annual report to the Securities and Exchange Commission, read the biographies of senior management. Which functional disciplines (such as marketing or finance) or business groups did they come from? Is there one unit or discipline that has contributed a disproportionately large share of senior managers (if so, that's where you want to be).

In a firm resume, don't read about the lawyers: read instead about the clients. Who are they, how healthy are they, and how long have they been a client? Is the firm overly dependent on a single client? If so, how strong is the firm's attachment to that client (are firm partners on the client's board of directors, for example)? If you are looking at a firm that is heavily dependent on one client for its business, you should research the client as if you were seeking employment there (for you are, in a way). As that client goes, so goes the firm. If the firm has many clients, is that because they are specialists in a particular area of practice? Patent and trademark firms will usually list many clients, but may not do anything for those clients outside the intellectual property field.

Similarly, investment banking clients normally spread their work among many law firms depending on their specialties -- Firm M will do the investment bank's real estate transactions, Firm N will do the public offerings, while Firm P will do the maritime and admiralty work. If you sense that the firm's reputation rests on a particular specialty, you had better want to specialize in that area of practice. Any specialty that is heavily dependent upon tax benefits from the federal or state governments should be scrutinized especially closely, as such a specialty can disappear overnight if there is a change in the tax laws.

  c. Talk to People Who Know the Employer From the Inside Out

Your best information about a prospective employer will not come from the written word, but rather from people. It is never too early nor too late to begin building up a personal network of contacts that can be sources of information not available to the general public. After all, this is where reporters and other journalists get their "scoops": why not you? Let's say you are interested in Firm X; how do you go about finding out what really goes on there? Who ya gonna call?

i.   *Alumni/ae*

First, you should visit or call your law school's placement office (even if it has been some time since you graduated). They will usually have their alumni/ae listed on a computerized data base, and can (for a small charge, or for free) give you the names, addresses and telephone numbers of any law school alumni/ae who work at Firm X and other similar firms in the same city. You probably have already figured out that your college placement office can furnish you with similar information about graduates of that college.

If there are no alumni/ae working at Firm X, what about one of Firm X's key clients? If you really want to see someone at a law firm jump to attention, call and indicate to his secretary that an executive of one of his important clients suggested you call.

here are no alumni/ae working at Firm X or one of Firm X's clients, how about one of Firm X's rival firms in that city (I would define a "rival firm" as a firm of comparable size, doing the same sort of work for the same sort of clientele). Who knows? If you succeed in impressing a lawyer at a rival firm, the latter may think to himself "gee, why should Firm X get all the hot prospects?", and you may find yourself interviewing at the rival firm!

ii.   Bar Association Contacts

Take a look at Martindale-Hubbell and see if there is a
local or regional bar association in which most of Firm X's
lawyers participate. If there is (and there usually will be), call
the bar association, find out which committees are most likely to
have lawyers from Firm X in your desired area of specialty (for
example, if you are interesting in representing banks, you will
probably want to talk to lawyers on the business/commercial
law committee), and then find out if there are any college or
law school alumni/ae participating in those committees.

iii.   Friends and Relatives

Finally, let's not overlook the obvious: that personal
friends, relatives of personal friends, family members and their
friends may also be useful sources of contacts at Firm X, one of
its clients, or one of its rivals.

iv.   Legal Recruiters or "Headhunters"

You should find out which legal recruiters -- or "head-
hunters" as they are commonly known -- work in the city
where Firm X is located, and ask them about Firm X's reputation in the marketplace. You will be surprised how much these
people know; lawyers at firms throughout the city are daily
telling them their tales of joy or woe. You will also be surprised how much the recruiters will tell you; since lawyers
change jobs fairly frequently these days, you are a potential
source of business to them. They may even be able to introduce you to someone who just recently left Firm X for greener
pastures, who will be only too willing to tell you more than you
ever wanted to know about Firm X and how they treat their

people (you should keep in mind, of course, that such a person is not likely to be very objective about Firm X, especially if he left under less-than-ideal circumstances). You are not asking the recruiters to help you find a job at Firm X; you are merely asking for help in networking through to someone who can answer some specific questions about Firm X, its practice and reputation in the legal community.

v.   Other Job Candidates

Finally, you should ask others who are looking for jobs in the same area what they have heard about Firm X. Of course, these people have no incentive to help you in your networking; they may even view you as a competitor and steer you away from opportunities which they may be pursuing. Nonetheless, I think it is worth a try, especially if you latch onto someone who is willing to swap information about Firm X for information about an employer you have researched in which he is interested.

d.   When You Find a Good Contact,
What Do You Say?

What should you say when asking a total stranger about Firm X? You should be very careful what you say, because you don't know this person, and if you don't know a person, you don't know who that person knows. This person you are talking to may be the golfing buddy of the chairperson of the Legal Hiring Committee at Firm X!

First, you should identify yourself and the reason for your call. Nothing is more frustrating to a busy attorney, no matter how senior or junior, than to receive a telephone call from a total stranger in a far-off city asking for information about a firm on the other side of town. Most people will take the time to be helpful, but only if you are straightforward with them. You should say "this will only take five (or ten) minutes", and then stick to your deadline unless the other person takes you over the limit. You should say that you are merely looking to learn something about Firm X and its local reputation, and that you are not calling with any ulterior motive (such as obtaining a job at the contact's employer).

Second, this is an "information interview", not a job interview, so you can be somewhat more demanding of the contact than you would a lawyer-interviewer from the target employer. Ask the questions whose answers you really want to know, and don't be afraid to ask for "gossip". Show that you know something about the target employer and its practice or business, so as to discourage the contact from merely reciting the "party line". If the contact is not very helpful, ask (in a polite and nice way) if he would be willing to introduce you to someone else in his organization who has had more direct contact with your target employer than perhaps he has had; you could suggest that perhaps there is someone in his organization who has worked at Firm X in the past, or has recently negotiated a transaction on the other side of Firm X's attorneys.

Be sure to express vigorously your thanks for any scrap of information he may deign to throw you, and follow up with a "thank you" letter even if he has not been very helpful. Once you have found employment, be sure to send him your business card and a short note letting him know how helpful he was in helping you "sort out your thinking".

e.   *"Networking" As a Way of Life*

Difficult as it is to call total strangers and ask for information, it is something you must become accustomed to. The process known as "networking" is probably the most productive way to obtain (legally) nonpublic information about any person or organization you are interested in contacting for any reason. Keep in mind that the shoe may be on the other foot someday; your contact may be calling you for assistance, and you will be obligated to do whatever you can. Also keep in mind that even if your "networking" proves to be unproductive, whether you know it or not you are polishing your interviewing skills with these faceless "contacts" in a nonthreatening way: nothing is at stake, and the worst they can do is hang up on you (few will). Even if you do not get what you want out of them, they will be flattered that you called, and if you stay in touch with them you may find there will come a time in your career when they are in the best possible position to help you.

One final rule of "networking" etiquette: while you should (indeed must) use the information you have obtained through networking in the job interview itself (to show your enthusiasm for the position and the thoroughness of your research), you must never disclose the name of the person who furnished you with that information. Attorneys are known for their discretion; while the lawyer-interviewer may be dying to know how you found out about the firm's growing municipal bond practice in State X and close ties to gubernatorial candidate Smith, like a good investigative reporter you must protect your sources. A good way to handle this is to say something like "well, good news gets around fast," and then follow up with a question of your own to get off the subject.

C.   Sizing Up The Interviewer(s)

Finding out what the target employer is really like, and obtaining nonpublic information that you can use to your advantage during the job interview itself, is only half the battle. To be truly successful in a legal job interview, and stand out from the crowd of people competing against you, it is necessary to know something about your lawyer-interviewer(s) before you walk in the door.

1.   Step One: Know "Who's Who in the Zoo"

The first stop is your law school placement office. By obtaining a copy of the firm resume or corporate materials that are on file there, you will be able to tell at a glance who the members of the firm's Legal Personnel Committee are, the names of the other attorneys in the corporation's legal department (and, more importantly, who reports to whom within the organization), and the division heads of the legal staff of the government agency.

You must keep in mind that not all lawyers employed by an organization will be lawyer-interviewers; only a very select handful will be chosen to perform this task, and your first task must be to identify the subset of lawyer-interviewers that lurks within the larger pool of attorneys employed by the target organization. Lawyer-interviewers will generally fall into one of two categories: either they are members of a Legal Personnel Committee or other select group of lawyers to whom the organization delegates the delicate task of screening candidates for employment; or they are lawyers to whom you will directly report if you are hired at the target organization.

Finding out the names of the lawyers to whom you would report if you are hired is relatively simple; usually the job description will contain this information, as in the case of a newspaper ad that says "reports to the Assistant General Counsel in charge of patents and trademarks". In the case of a "lateral hire" or career change, however, this information may not be as easily obtained. In these cases you will have to call the target employer's personnel office and find out verbally who heads up the XYZ division's legal staff, or who the senior partners in the firm's Bankruptcy Department are. Sometimes you will not be able to find out this all-important information until the initial interview; in this case one of your first questions for the lawyer-interviewer should be "how is the department structured, and who reports to whom within the department?"

If you are interviewing for your first legal job out of law school, virtually all of your interviews will be with members of the Legal Personnel Committee. Finding out who these people are should be as easy as looking at the firm resume on file in your law school placement office. If this information is not available, the placement office personnel should be able to get it for you (and for your competition) without much difficulty, or you may wish to call the firm's recruitment coordinator and obtain the information directly. There is a risk, of course, in taking the latter course, as if you identify yourself to the recruitment coordinator he may be tempted to tell a member of the Committee to "be careful when talking to So-and-So from Law School X; he's been calling here asking all kinds of questions." As in so many other aspects of the information gathering process, your ability to be discreet counts for much here.

One way to do this is to call the firm, ask for the recruitment coordinator's secretary (not the coordinator himself) and, without identifying yourself, say that you are interested in writing a letter to the Chairman of the Legal Personnel Committee and want to know the correct spelling of his name. At least you will know one name through this method. Another way of achieving your goal is to make friends with a librarian at another law firm in the same city; it is my experience that law librarians all know each other, and if he likes you he may be willing to place a discreet telephone call to his counterpart at the target firm and ask for a list of the Legal Personnel Committee members.

2.   *Step Two: Learn About Individual Interviewers*

Once you have found the names of the Legal Personnel Committee members and the most influential partners in the department or division in which you will be working if hired, your task is a simple one: find out as much about each one of them as you possibly can before you walk into his office. As will be seen, this is a process that continues right up to the moment (and sometimes after) the interview begins.

a.   *His Curriculum Vitae*

The first stop, of course, is Martindale-Hubbell. There you will find the individual's date of birth, educational history (where he graduated from college and law school and years of graduation), a list of publications and bar memberships, professional honors and awards, and (sometimes) area of practice concentration. If you are looking at a corporate legal department or government agency, the Prentice-Hall Directory of Corporate Counsel may be a better place to start, as more corporations list detailed information about their legal staff there than they do in Martindale-Hubbell.

b.   *Common Interests in the Law*

If you find that the lawyer-interviewer you are research-ing has written a number of articles for law reviews or bar journals, should you read any or all of them prior to the inter-view? My advice is usually no; it takes up too much time, you probably won't remember much of importance (and will risk misquoting the article when actually speaking to the lawyer-interviewer), and you will appear to be "brown-nosing" if you show any detailed familiarity with the interviewer's written work. You should, however, know the titles of the articles he has written, and if you have the time you should read the brief synopsis or "executive summary" that usually appears at the beginning of each article.

This will give you an idea of the particular issues or problems in which the interviewer is interested, and if you can (sincerely and genuinely) make the connection between the interviewer's interest and something you yourself have written about or studied, so much the better. The key words here are "genuinely" and "sincerely"; if the lawyer-interviewer thinks you are coming across as too polished, or are trying to "brown nose" him, he may be tempted to turn the tables on you by asking a series of detailed (and embarrassing) questions to find out just how closely you have followed his work.

What are you looking for, then, in studying the inter-viewer's biography? You are looking for something in com-mon. If the interviewer is a graduate of your college or law school, or has written extensively in an area you are currently writing your Law Review note or case comment about, or shares a charitable or political interest or hobby, you have something to talk about that will set you apart from the competition. Rarely will Martindale-Hubbell and the other legal directories give you all of the information you will need to know in a legal job interview.

c.   *The Really Good Stuff*

To get the "really good stuff" about a lawyer-interviewer, you must resort to networking and "gossip", just as you did when researching the target employer. Talking to other attorneys in the community can be very useful here if you are in a "lateral hire" or career changing situation; while professionals are notoriously uneasy about tattling on their colleagues in the bar, most will give you a balanced presentation of the "scuttlebutt" if they feel they can trust you to be discreet. Keep in mind that you are not trying to find out about the lawyer-interviewer's sex life or personal idiosyncrasies, the sort of things people are naturally reluctant to talk about.

You are trying to find out harmless things: his hobbies, number of children, political or community interests, professional interests (bar association committees and the like), significant cases or business transactions he is known for, client contacts, and so forth. When you have learned something about an interviewer that you think will help you establish rapport with him, write down a question that you think will help "open him up" on an area of mutual interest or concern and get him talking away about something the two of you find fascinating.

d.   *Study the Interviewer's Office*

Finally, keep your eyes open when you walk into the interview room (or the interviewer's office). If you arrive for the interview a couple of minutes early, and (lucky you!) are asked to wait in the office for a couple of minutes as the interviewer has been detained in a meeting, look around you and drink in every detail. Are there paintings of sailboats on the wall? What sorts of legal and nonlegal books are on the bookshelf? If there are bound volumes or "lucites" anywhere in the office, what types of transactions or cases were they and how much money was at stake? Are there any memorabilia or toys on the interviewer's desk? What does the furniture look like -- contemporary (metal and glass), traditional (solid hardwoods), or beat up (passed on from partner to partner over the generations)?

Look at the inevitable pictures of the interviewer's family -- are the children holding any objects (like a baseball glove) that may offer clues to their parent's hobbies or interests? Do the family pictures face the interviewer, or is his back turned to them? Is the interviewer's desk tidy or disorganized? Is there a "wall" of paper separating you from the interviewer, or is everything off to one side? Does the interviewer's desk face toward the window or the door?

Little details like these can speak volumes about a person, and you should be attentive to them every minute you are interviewing. Even when you have not been given an opportunity to size up the interviewer's desk and office before the interview, you should take advantage of every moment during the interview to do so. By using the techniques described in Chapter 4, you will have plenty of time to make the necessary assessments. I cannot hold myself out as a psychologist or expert on "body language" or utilization of space, but by using common sense you can usually determine from the arrangement of a person's office or desk how compulsive he is, how important his family life is to him, what he does with his spare time, and the type of work that means the most to him.

Two things you should never do when in an interviewer's office: open up any of his desk drawers; or go behind his desk to look at something at closer range. The former is an invasion of privacy, the latter is viewed by most people as an invasion of the interviewer's "personal space" that he may well resent.

e.   The Interviewer's Appearance

Finally, when you greet the interviewer make a detailed note of his appearance. How well (and how conservatively) does he dress? Is his presentation formal or informal? Does he ramble on or watch every word? How does he use his space -- does he keep the desk between you and him or do the two of you sit on the same side of the desk? Does he make regular eye contact or is he looking through you?

You should keep in mind that employers pick their lawyer-interviewers because they are exemplars of what the employer wants in its lawyers -- indeed, one of the surest ways to spot the up-and-coming lawyers in an organization is to see which ones are named to the Legal Personnel Committee. Ask yourself constantly during the interview: do I want to be like him someday? That is the question your prospective employer wants you to ask: if the answer is "no", you need try to impress the interviewer no further.

CHAPTER 4

CONDUCTING YOURSELF IN
A LEGAL JOB INTERVIEW

A.   *Introduction: How Not To Conduct A Legal
     Job Interview*

You have now passed the preliminary hurdles in the
legal job interviewing process. You have researched the
employer and the interviewer(s), you have a long list of questions which you have carefully memorized, and you have done
something (such as answering an advertisement, contacting a
headhunter, or signing up in your law school placement office)
that has made the employer want to interview you for a position. You are now on your way to the interviewer's office, or
one of the airless cubicles in your law school placement office
(why is it that so many placement offices are located in the law
school basement?), where the interview is going to take place.

What should be going through your mind as you walk in
the door? How should you conduct yourself during the interview? What should you do with your hands? Your feet?
Should you look the interviewer in the eye or at a point three
inches above his head? How much talking should you do?
How much talking should the interviewer do? What is the best
way to close the interview? Do you have to send a thank-you
note afterwards?

To combine all of these questions in a single question:
how do you put my best foot forward and maximize the
chances of making a positive impression on this fellow human
being whom fate has thrown into the same room with me for a

few brief but precious minutes? This chapter helps you answer this most important of all interviewing questions.

Before we begin our dissection of the legal job interview, it may be wise to take a quick and humorous look at how not to interview for a legal position. A friend of mine tells this story, and it is one of my personal favorites:

I wasn't one of the brightest in my law school class, but I wasn't one of the dumbest either! I was interviewing for a summer clerkship with a large law firm, so of course I knew I was up against some tough competition. Some of those guys can be pretty condescending too, especially if your law school isn't Harvard or Yale. But I never knew the meaning of condescension until I interviewed one day with a lawyer from a prominent firm from a medium-size city in the Midwest (to avoid any libel of an otherwise excellent firm and a very liveable city, I am calling it "Midwest City").

I had signed up to interview with the Midwest City firm out of curiosity more than anything else. It was the only Midwest City firm that interviewed at my law school that year, I had some distant relatives who lived in Midwest City, and frankly I was dating someone who was originally from that area. I just wanted to find out if firms in the Midwest were any more laid back than firms in the Northeast, with the thought that if I liked these guys enough I might be willing to split my summer; I noted that I was one of only three people who had signed up to interview for the firm, none of them Law Review or top ten percent, so I thought my chances for a "call back" were pretty good.

The interviewer from the Midwest City firm was one of the senior partners: a tougher, more ornery looking bird I have never seen before or since. He glared at me when I walked into the interview room, perused my resume briefly, let it drop to the floor, and then sat back, crossed his arms, and began to interrogate me with some of the most pointed, offensive questions I have ever been asked in an interview setting. If my grades were so good in college, how come I didn't go to Harvard? Why had I done so poorly in Contracts first semester? Why wasn't I a member of the Order of the Coif (a national honor society for law students; to be a member one must be in the top ten percent of one's class)? Why hadn't I been selected for Law Review? Why wasn't I looking at less prestigious firms, since it was clear I didn't have what it took to be seriously considered by a firm like his? Why was I talking to a firm from Midwest City when it was clear I hadn't any prior connection to the city?

After a few minutes I began to get angry; I held back at first, because I thought this was the "adversary interview" that all of the books on interviewing talk about, and I wanted to demonstrate that I was tough and could defend a difficult case (this particular partner, I found out later, was one of the top trial lawyers at his firm, and so was probably pretty accustomed to cross-examination). Perhaps he was trying to "test" me to see if I could handle a difficult situation.

But with each passing minute it became more and more clear that he was not playing an interviewing game with me: he was sincerely offended that someone with my less-than-stellar credentials had applied to interview with his firm, he quite clearly believed that someone like me should not even be considering a career in law, and he wanted to do everything in *his power to put me down and punish me for my boldness. Finally, after what seemed like a hailstorm of fire and brimstone, in the form of one "negative" question after another, he interrupted my answer in midstream, threw his notepad down on the floor (he had not taken a single note that I saw), folded his arms, turned away from me, and said "okay, I've heard all I need to know. Now, what do you want to know about the firm?"*

At this point I was too mad to speak. I was as close to physically assaulting someone as I ever hope to get in my life. I decided that I wasn't going to blow up and give him the satisfaction of knowing that his judgment about me was correct. But I wasn't going to let him get away with his rude behavior either. Knowing that nothing I could do would interest him in me (and having decided that I wouldn't work in his firm if they paid the highest starting salary in the United States), I calmly pulled out a small notepad and pen from my jacket pocket, poised myself to jot down notes, and asked the partner "tell me, Mr. So-and-So, I see from Martindale-Hubbell that you went to Harvard Law School. Tell me, what was your rank in class?"

The partner almost fell out of his chair. He turned to face me, stunned, and asked in bold disbelief, "why is that of any importance to you?" I said "Well, to be honest yours is the first firm outside the Northeast I've interviewed with. I'm looking primarily at firms in the Northeast, because everyone knows the quality of practice there is so much better than it is anywhere else, if not necessarily the quality of life. I'm curious to find out how much of a tradeoff in quality in practice I'll have to make if I settle for your firm." The partner began to turn red, and sputtered "I'll have you know, I was in the top quarter of my class at Harvard." "Thank you," I said, and jotted the

_information down on my pad, asking as I wrote "and were you
a member of the Harvard Law Review?" His eyes widened as
if I had pulled a knife on him. "No, I wasn't, but I was editor of
one of the other journals there; you could have known that had
you read Martindale-Hubbell." "I know, sir, but then I also
knew that you were not Order of the Coif so you could not
have been in the top ten percent of your class either," I said._

_"Now tell me," I continued, "did you go directly to
your present law firm? Or was there a stop in between? Did
you start somewhere else?" The partner couldn't believe his
ears; he was clearly amazed, but instead he sat back in his chair,
squirming at the taste of his own medicine, and said "no; I went
directly to this firm." "Did you look at law firms elsewhere?"
"No, I didn't." "Why didn't you? You're not a native of
Midwest City, and you didn't go to college there." (I knew this
from Martindale-Hubbell). "I don't think I have to answer
that."_

_Now I had him. I threw my notepad down on the floor,
directly on top of his, took off my glasses very slowly, looked
him straight in the eye, and said, "Mr. So-and-So, there's a lot
here that just does not fit. If you were in the top quarter of your
class at Harvard, a journal editor to boot, you could have gone
anywhere in the country to practice law. What the Devil are
you doing in Midwest City?" The partner turned beet red, and
his hands started clutching the armrests on his chair as if he
were holding himself back. I sat back in my chair and said, "I
don't see any point in continuing this discussion; you see, I care
as much as you do about working with quality lawyers. And in
treating me the way you have in the past few minutes you have
just turned off the best summer clerk you are ever going to get
from this law school this year. Because only three students_

signed up to interview with your firm, and I'm the best of them. Anybody who's better -- in your definition of better -- wouldn't be caught dead talking to a firm from Midwest City when they know they can work for a firm from New York, or Washington D.C., or San Francisco. I can think of only two reasons that might explain your decision to practice law in Midwest City: either you were dating someone from there, which as it so happens I am right now, or you just couldn't get into anyplace better. Next time, before you tear into someone, try to remember that beggars can't be choosers."

I didn't give him the chance to respond; by this point he was furious, quaking with anger, and was trying to keep from becoming physically violent, much as I had earlier in the interview. I picked up my pad, turned my back on this loser, and stormed out. I didn't have too much of a chance to gloat about my "turnabout is fair play" treatment of the interviewer, though. For there, waiting to interview with that same monster, was one of my best friends in law school, who happened to hail from Midwest City. This interview obviously meant a great deal to him, and I felt lousy the rest of the day knowing that I had set him up for one of the worst experiences of his life (although, frankly, I don't have any assurance that the interviewer would have treated him any differently). When I saw my friend later that evening, he said "What did you say to that guy? I couldn't get a word out of him the first couple of minutes; I thought he was going to have a stroke!"

I am sure many of you had a twinge of satisfaction in reading my friend's account of a particularly nasty interview. There are two morals, however, to this story, neither of them favorable to my friend. While many lawyers are fine examples of humanity, the legal profession like any other has its share of

jerks, bastards and other difficult people. Learning to survive in
a legal job environment means learning to deal with all kinds of
personality types, egos and political styles. Later on in this
chapter we will discuss dealing with the difficult interviewer.

What is more important, though, is the effect that my
friend's conduct had on the entire interviewing process: by his
own admission, he hurt one of his best friends in law school
without intending to. Even more serious, he may have poi-
soned his law school's reputation with that law firm; if I were
that interviewer, with the titanic ego he had, I would have recommended to my Legal Personnel Committee that we write
that law school off for good. If the law school's Placement
Director (or Dean) heard about my friend's conduct from the
interviewer or from other alumni/ae who were working at that
firm, I think my friend's reputation would have been in jeop-
ardy, and he may have been cut out of the interviewing pro-
gram (these sorts of things routinely happen, although they did
not happen to my friend).

One thing I have learned in my years of practicing law:
no matter how large the profession may seem (just look at the
size of those Martindale-Hubbell volumes, after all), you are
constantly bumping into people you've worked with, people
you've interviewed with, people you went to law school with,
people you negotiated or litigated against, over and over again.
You cannot afford to alienate anyone you encounter in your
practice, even if it makes you feel good at the time. Perhaps
this explains why some of the most successful lawyers alive
today have the blandest and most colorless of personalities:
they don't light any fires, but they don't create any negative
impressions either! With that in mind, let's begin our discussion
of the legal job interview.

B.   Your Mindset As You Walk In The Door

It is so easy to "blow" an important interview before it is even started. Too many job candidates are so eager to "get down to business" that they forget an interview is as much a social occasion as a business one: your first task, and perhaps your only task, is to get the interviewer to like you as a person.

If a person likes you, he is usually willing to overlook an occasional slight or faux-pas, and is more likely to give you the benefit of the doubt in chancy situations. As the social psychologists tell us, likes usually are attracted to likes (or more precisely, people are attracted to other people whom they perceive to be like themselves, regardless of the actual truth), and people are more likely to think good things about (and do good things for) people whom they find attractive. This is not limited to physical attractiveness, although being considered extremely attractive in the physical sense cannot hurt your chances of winning an interviewer over.

Most books on interviewing stress the importance of "making a good first impression" when you walk in the interviewer's door, and give a few basic, commonsense rules for beginning a job interview:
- --   relax;
- --   don't appear to be overly eager or artificially enthusiastic;
- --   don't appear to be worried or under pressure to get a job quickly (or "never let them see you sweat");
- --   be pleasant but not to the point where you might appearto be obsequious or "smarmy";

--   greet the interviewer with a smile and a firm
        (but not bone-crushing) handshake;

and so forth. This is all well and good, but what the interview
books don't tell you is "how to do it". When you are interviewing for a job you really want, and when there is much at
stake (say, for example, you have been out of work for several
months, the severance pay from your old employer has run out,
and your spouse is nagging you about the mortgage payment
that is due the first of next month), it is very difficult indeed for
your mind to tell your stomach and your nerve endings to "calm
down; it's only an interview; it's not your life".

Rather than waste time focusing on your general demeanor or image as you walk into the interview room (we will
talk about that in the next section), let us focus instead on your
mindset -- what is going through your mind as you walk into the
room and greet the interviewer.

It is my experience that you cannot control your feelings
at a given moment; if you are thinking sad thoughts you cannot
help but feel sad. By changing your thoughts, however, you
can manipulate your feelings -- how you perceive an event is as
important (and sometimes, as we will see, more important) as
the event itself. Politicians and their advisors often resort to
"spin control" -- presenting an event in the light most favorable
to the politician or the light least favorable to his adversaries --
in order to manipulate the public's perception of the politician
and his policy goals. You, too, can (and should) resort to "spin
control" to put your thoughts in the light most favorable to you
before you begin a legal job interview; your feelings will
follow your positive thoughts naturally and you will present a
positive image to the interviewer. Let us see how it is done.

Rule # 1: Make Believe You Already Have The Job

This rule is not as outrageous as it sounds at first, for in a way, you may have already passed the biggest hurdle in winning a legal job before you walk into the first interview. If you are applying for an advertised or posted position, or if you have made a contact through networking or through a headhunter, your potential employer has reviewed your resume, screened your credentials, and decided that your background and experience fit the job. Otherwise, why would the company or firm waste time interviewing you?

Sometimes the only question remaining at that point is whether you are better suited for the job than the others who have also passed this initial screening along with you. In other words, the company or firm has already "screened out" those whose credentials and experience are clearly not a "fit" for the job; what is now necessary is to "screen in" the candidate to whom an offer will be made (with perhaps a backup), and "screen out" the rest.

In such a situation your mindset walking into the interview should be "I've already got the job; my credentials and experience are a fit, otherwise why would they be wasting their time on me? I won't spend a lot of time rehashing my resume, and I won't ever be defensive about anything on my resume, because in all likelihood they have already figured out they can live with whatever weaknesses there may be in my background."

You have all heard about sports teams who go into a big game where they are highly favored over their opponents:

about such a team it is often said that "the game is theirs to lose", meaning that if they can keep their spirits up, maintain momentum and discipline at all times, and make a sincere effort to win, they should be able to do so easily. If, on the other hand, the favored team gets lazy, allows itself to be "psyched out" by the other team, or otherwise loses their discipline or momentum during the game, they stand a good chance of losing the game even though the other team isn't deserving of a victory.

You should think the same about yourself going into the "big game" of a legal job interview: "the job is already mine; I can only lose it by fouling up -- by saying or doing something that turns the interviewer off or by revealing a significant weakness that the interviewer has no cause to suspect." We will examine some of the most common "foulups" in subsequent sections; the important thing now is to remember that when walking into a legal job interview you must not be overly concerned on "selling" yourself, like a telephone salesperson trying to sell you real estate in a swampland somewhere, but rather on not saying or doing anything that may cause the interviewer to think you are not a "fit" for the job.

Be assured, the interviewer is not on your side in this effort; he is looking for you to make such a mistake, because it makes his job much easier (you will recall from Chapter 2 that this is the interviewer's primary goal: to make a decision he can easily defend in the shortest possible time and with the least amount of inconvenience or effort). The candidate who says or does something that turns the interviewer off effectively "screens himself out" of the competition, even though he may have the best credentials for the job, and even though he may in reality be the most perfect "fit". Some interviewers go out of their way to try to surface such "screening out" information during an interview, and you must be sure at all times that the interviewer does not succeed!

Life is not fair this way: often (in fact, I think most of the time) the winner in a legal job interview is not the best qualified candidate in fact, but simply the one who performed the best during the interviewing process. In other words, the victor is not often he who is best, but he who has made the fewest mistakes (and isn't that after all a prime quality of the good lawyer -- that he doesn't make mistakes when representing a client in court, or drafting a legal document, or negotiating a delicate business transaction)? As a friend of mine -- who does a lot of interviewing for his firm -- puts it: "sometimes we pick a person out of the pack simply because we can't think of anything bad to say about him, even though we're not wildly enthusiastic about him, if we can indeed say bad things about the other candidates."

Rule # 1 is not in itself a guarantee of success in a legal job interview. If after several interviews there remain several candidates, none of whom has made an interviewing mistake or otherwise "screened himself out", the interviewer(s) must still make a decision and pick one. The result at that point may be a popularity contest, or may hinge on an individual's unique strength in an area of critical importance to the job. Rule # 1 is, however, a guarantee that you will make it to the "final cut" and be among those so considered.

There is an exception to Rule # 1, which applies when you have signed up at your law school placement office to interview with a firm for your first legal job (be it a summer clerkship or your first job upon graduation). While you may be

required to deposit your resume with the placement director a
week or two before the interview date, usually the interviewer
does not "pre-screen" the resume, and may be going into the
interview with absolutely no idea of your credentials, background or experience.

In such a situation you really cannot assume going in
that you already have the job; indeed you will probably spend
most of the interview reviewing the items on your resume with
the intent of demonstrating your "fit" for the job and the employer. If your grades are not up to snuff, or you are not a
"Law Review type", you will probably be screened out before
the interview even begins.

A better approach to follow in this situation is to tell
yourself that for a specific type of employer (large firm, small
firm, corporate legal department), "all entry-level positions are
alike", that one opportunity is as good as another, and it will
only be a matter of time before you find a situation that will
play to your strengths. There is an element of self-deception in
this, but keep in mind that what you tell yourself is merely a
"tool" designed to help you calm yourself down and keep the
interviewing process in perspective, and make a good first
impression on the interviewer. Whether or not you internalize
these beliefs after the interview is over is not important, because by then they will have served their purpose; they have
prevented you from looking like an uptight, worried, neurotic
dweeb during the interview.

*Rule # 2: Weave A Safety Net For Yourself, Even If
You Have To Weave It Out Of Thin Air*

What about the feeling that you are under pressure to
succeed in the interview? Or the feeling that "if I don't get this
job it will be absolutely horrible -- I'll end up on Skid Row?"
Too much attention to these thoughts will make you appear
anxious, worried, and pressured, and the interviewer will be
turned off before you even open your mouth to say "good
morning."

Anxiety is Catching. When you appear anxious, you
make other people feel anxious; I have discovered that people
are generally more responsive to your moods and feelings than
you think. Have you noticed that whenever you are in a conversation with someone and you start talking faster and faster,
they start talking faster and faster too? The same is true of
emotions; if you appear awkward, you will make the interviewer feel ill at ease and he will sooner or later begin to
appear awkward. The interviewer does not enjoy this feeling
of being awkward, he inwardly blames you for producing that
feeling, and he will screen you out.

The "Dating Game", Then and Now. More importantly, it is one of the great ironies of interviewing that the
candidates who display that they really need the job are never
the ones who get it. Those of you who are young enough to
remember dating in high school or college will know how this
goes: was there ever someone in your life (usually it was not a
physically attractive someone) who developed a crush on you
and followed you everywhere you went, making a nuisance of
himself or herself trying to get your attention, and doing everything within his or her power short of committing a felony to get

you to go out with him or her? If there was, tell me, how interested were you in that person? If you are like most people, you wouldn't have anything to do with such a person.

Did you ever stop to think that that person would do anything for your affection, be more true and loyal to you than anyone else, and return your affection tenfold until the day he or she died? I'll bet you actually did at some point or other. But you still weren't interested, were you, you soulless heart-breaker? Instead of settling for the one you could get without lifting a finger, you spent your time (more or less discreetly) trying to get the attention of someone who wouldn't even give you the time of day -- the handsomest guy on the football team, the prettiest cheerleader, , the Homecoming King or Queen. And, pray tell, how did he or she treat you? Probably just the same way you were treating the poor slob who was tagging along after you everyplace with his or her tongue hanging down to his or her knees.

It is much the same with interviewing. The candidate who is most likely to get a job interview is the one the interviewer most likes but is not completely certain he can get; the candidate he is least interested in is the one who fawns all over him and sends him a signal that he would do anything to get the job. Why this is I don't know; I'm not enough of a psychologist to have figured it out. But it is a fact of interviewing life: the more you are perceived to want or need a job, the less your chances of getting it.

The Need for a "Poker Face". Another possible reason, which should not be overlooked, is that the law is not a very emotional business. A lawyer is expected to remain calm and detached at all times; this puts clients at ease, since if a lawyer looks worried, the client sees a jail cell or the poorhouse in his future. Lawyers are uncomfortable generally with people who display their emotions or who otherwise show that they cannot control their feelings. If a candidate appears overly eager, or overly anxious, an interviewer is likely to think to himself "gee, if this person gets so wound up about a lousy job interview, can you imagine how he'll be in a tough courtroom situation? How will he deal with some of our crazier clients?"

This is not to say that you should send signals that you are not interested in the job you are interviewing for. Heaven forbid! That would be an instant "screen out" of the type you want to avoid at all costs. It does mean, however, that you have to stifle a certain amount of your enthusiasm for the job or the employer, even at the risk of appearing a trifle distant or luke-warm.

One way to calm your fears that I have found very successful is to "weave yourself a safety net." It will be much easier for you to believe (sincerely) that winning the job is not the most important thing in your life if you can persuade yourself that you do in fact have other options -- that there is always something else you can do if all else fails and you don't get a job offer from anyone in the world.

In my own case, I worked a few years as a reporter for a major metropolitan daily newspaper before I started law school. That was years ago, but whenever I find myself thinking that a job interview is a "do or die" situation I calm myself down by telling myself that if all else fails I can always go back to that newspaper (or another one) and write obituaries or feature articles for a while.

Now, I haven't the foggiest idea if I could in fact do such a thing; I probably would be considered overqualified for such a position by this time. But this "little white lie" that I have told myself does me a great deal of good; I usually do calm down and keep the interview in better perspective, and as a result I appear more calm and relaxed, which puts the interviewer at ease and makes me appear more professional and mature.

This "little white lie" is what I mean when I say that you should weave a safety net for yourself "even if you have to weave it out of thin air." Think about something you would really like to do, that is possible for you to do without a great deal of money or inconvenience -- start a small business out of your home, for example, or become a late-night disk jockey for your local radio station (talking and playing records for a living -- I'm sure you could do it), or write legal articles for your local newspaper. Forget for the moment that the job wouldn't pay a decent living wage; just concentrate on picking something that you could do well without much effort, that would give you an entry-level position without much effort, and that would be fun to do for a while. Once you have found it, make it your "safety net", write it down on a little piece of paper, stick it in your wallet or purse (in a place where you can reach it easily and scan it while waiting for the interview to begin), and keep saying to yourself "I'm not making a big deal of this; it would be nice to get the job, but if all else fails, I can always do X -- I will not end up on the streets rummaging through garbage pails for my supper." Just don't fall too much in love with your "safety net" position, or you may just decide to give up practicing law altogether!

Rule # 3: "Warm, Friendly, Smile, Low-Key"

This is really a collection of rules, a mantra that I repeat over and over to myself just before walking into a legal job interview. I have found it helpful in developing the right frame of mind, which in turn affects the "image" I present to the interviewer in a very positive manner. Let us look at each element of Rule # 3 in turn.

Warm. It should go without saying that you should not come across as a cold fish. Your personal style should be warm and inviting, your stance relaxed without being limp. Your facial expression and body language should communicate to the interviewer, "look, I am genuinely interested in this position, but I don't look upon this interview as a stressful situation, and neither should you; so let's get down to the business of getting to know each other."

Friendly. Without showing too much of your personality, you should signal to the interviewer that you genuinely like him, that you are the sort of person who would get along with just about anybody and win them over. As in other professions and walks of life, loners generally do not succeed in the law; attracting and keeping clients requires as much "people skills" as technical lawyering skills, and no law firm or corporation wants to hire someone who will have to work behind closed doors all the time.

Smile. You should not forget to do this. Your smile should not be flashy or forced, but you must not forget to smile. Psychologists tell us that when we smile we unconsciously trigger happy thoughts and emotions that put our minds at ease; your actions in this regard do indeed influence your thoughts.

If you do not have a natural smile, develop one! If necessary, tell yourself a favorite joke or remind yourself of a humorous or silly situation from your past as you walk in the door: your slight laugh will come across as a natural smile.

Low-Key. This is the most important element of Rule # 3. You absolutely must not appear to be intense, uptight, or overly concentrated. You must send a signal to the interviewer that nothing really bothers you, and that while you work well under pressure, you never let the pressure get to you. Far from being a turn-off, this sort of emotional detachment from the situation is a very positive sign that you are a mature, mentally healthy, well adjusted professional. The trick is to present a low-key image without appearing to be bored or uninterested; one way to avoid appearing too "laid back" is to listen intently to the interviewer's every word, and make it a point not to sit too far back in your chair.

Once you have mastered Rule # 3, you must make a mantra of it. Just as the door of the interview room swings open, you should repeat to yourself "warm, friendly, smile, low-key" over and over again. During the interview, if the interviewer has launched on a lengthy monologue about his employer or a favorite "war story", you should occasionally repeat to yourself "warm, friendly, smile, low-key". Finally, as you stand to leave the interview room, or walk with the interviewer down the hall to your next interview, the phrase "warm, friendly, smile, low-key" should be foremost in your mind.

If it helps, another helpful mnemonic device that you can use to set yourself in the right frame of mind before a legal job interview is what I call the "four C's" -- Calm, Confidence, Courage, Control -- with "control" being the most important of these. Not only are you going to be in control of your emotions, fears and feelings, real or imagined, but you are also going to "control" the flow of information during the interview, in a way that will present you in the best possible light. You will learn the key ways of accomplishing this "control" over the interviewing process later in this chapter.

Rule # 4: Show A Personal Interest In The Interviewer

It is common for an inexperienced job candidate to begin an interview by rattling off every item on his resume, or giving the answer to an anticipated question that has not been asked yet (or may never be asked). While it is natural for you to want to "get down to business" quickly, you must repress this natural desire as by giving in to it you send the interviewer an invisible signal that you want to "get this over with quickly" or worse yet, that you are an intense, self-absorbed neurotic who does not know how to get along with people.

You must take the time to get to know the interviewer personally; if the interviewer does not buy you as a person, he is not about to buy you as a lawyer. If the interviewer begins talking as you walk in the door (most lawyer-interviewers will start the conversation), listen intently to what is being said and forget for a moment your prepared lead-in or initial question. See if you can't think of a follow-up question to ask; doing this successfully shows the interviewer you know how to listen, you are keenly interested in what he said (which cannot but impress him), and you are able to focus on the moment without following an internal "script". As we will see later in the chapter, the earlier you start directing the interview, the more likely it is you will succeed.

But what if the interviewer does not begin talking as you walk through the door, but instead just sits there in stony silence, looking at your resume or just staring at you? If you have done your research on the interviewer as described in Chapter 3, you should have found at least one common area of interest that you could use to begin the interview. I would begin by pointing out this area of interest and then asking a question based on it. For example, if your research has uncovered that the interviewer is an alumnus of your law school, you might say something like, "it must be interesting for you to come back to [Name of Law School] each year; do you see any differences or any changes taking place since you were here?" This is small talk, and accepted as such. But it shows that you are interested in the interviewer as a person without going out of your way to "brown nose" him, and it gets the conversation off to a relaxed start. Most importantly, it gets the interviewer to open up and start talking about something he cannot help but have something to say about.

Another approach is to highlight a shared interest, especially if you can do so by focusing on an object or event that is immediately present. For example, let's say that as you walk into the interviewer's office he is on the telephone talking to a client about a pending antitrust lawsuit. You have just taken an antitrust course and understand what the interviewer means when he refers on the telephone to a "possible Robinson-Patman claim." When the interviewer hangs up and apologizes for the delay, you may wish to say something like "no, not at all, in fact I was quite interested in what you were talking about. I'm working on a paper on the Robinson-Patman Act right now, and your conversation sounded interesting. If I may ask, what is that case about?"

Or, if you see a model of a sailboat on his desk, you may wish to begin the interview by saying "that model looks interesting; are you a sailor?" The interviewer will then have no choice but to talk about a hobby he no doubt dearly loves (if he is a sailor), or (if he is not a sailor) explain how the sailboat model comes to be sitting on his desk. Either way he will be talking about something that is of interest to him, and if you listen very carefully you will not have to worry about what to say next; his conversation will lead naturally to a follow-up question.

There is no better way to get someone to like you than to show (1) that you are interested in him as a person and are willing to spend some time getting to know him as a person before you "get down to business", and (2) that you share a common interest, goal or background. It bears repeating that human beings are attracted to people they perceive as being like themselves; throughout the interview you should be emphasizing how the two of you are really quite similar people, and downplay any significant differences (such as ethnic background or law school grade-point average) that may exist.

Rule # 5: Make 'Em Laugh

Let's face it, lawyers are not funny people. Their business is a serious one; when clients call their lawyers it is usually because they face a serious problem, or a legal liability, and they will usually have little time or patience for levity. Nonetheless, there are few better ways to "break the ice" than to get the interviewer to laugh. There is an old saying among criminal lawyers that "a laughing jury never convicts." Similarly, a laughing interviewer cannot help but think you are a clever person if you can make him laugh during what is for him a stressful experience.

You should be very careful, however, how you go about making the interviewer laugh. Telling jokes (especially off-color ones) will not go over very well. Rather, a well told humorous incident from your own past, especially one that highlights one of your personal or professional strengths, is the way to go. If your personality is such, however, that you are not comfortable with humor, it is best to avoid it altogether than risk making a fool of yourself.

Rule # 6: Warm Up For Your Audience

Before striding out on the stage of a comedy club or night spot, a stand-up comedian does not sit alone in his dressing room staring at the four walls. Instead, he will walk around, talking to the backstage hands and the other entertainers, talking about anything that may come into his head. He is not doing this for idle amusement; he is "warming up" for his act, putting himself at ease, exercising his vocal chords, and pumping a little bit of adrenalin, so that when he is announced and runs up on stage to take the microphone he appears to do so naturally and without an awkward pause in the flow of the evening's entertainment.

While you should not come across as a stand-up comedian during a legal job interview, this "warming up" technique is one you should consider using. You should not stand or sit in the waiting area silent, staring at the four walls. This will make you more nervous, as when you are idle you are more likely to be besieged by unwanted, negative, self-defeating thoughts. It is better to talk to someone -- anyone -- in a casual, lighthearted manner, as this takes your mind off the immensity of the task ahead of you, calms you down, and enables you to practice your "shtick" before an audience of people who are not sitting in judgment over you.

I find that secretaries and other clerical staff people are especially useful in this regard. If I am forced to wait outside the interviewer's office for a minute or two before the interview begins, I almost always strike up a conversation with the interviewer's secretary, asking questions about the office decor, the working environment, items on his desk that reveal a shared interest, and so forth.

If I am lucky, the secretary will reveal something about her boss' work habits, or his schedule that day, that will provide me with a much-needed "opener" for the interview. I may, if I am really lucky, learn something about the interviewer that will help me decide if I want the job or not. I once was having such a conversation with the secretary of a man who was going to interview me, and at one point she said, "you know, would it be possible for you to wait another minute or two? His wife has been trying to reach him all day and I've had her on hold for fifteen minutes." In my view, any person who does not return his spouse's telephone calls promptly, and/or keeps his spouse on hold for indefinite periods, is not a person for whom I would like to work. This secretary's boss did not help matters by ushering me into his office, apologizing for the delay, and (when I suggested that he may wish first to take any telephone calls that may be on hold) saying "oh, don't worry about that flashing light; I know who it is, and it can wait."

C.   *Your Professional Appearance*

Before you open your mouth in a legal job interview, the interviewer will have an opportunity (however brief) to see how you look, how you dress, how you walk, and how you carry yourself. Since first impressions are lasting ones, you need to be very concerned about those fleeting first moments when the interviewer is "sizing you up." This is not a "Dress for Success" book by any means, and you should follow closely the suggestions made by John Molloy in his two classic books -- Dress for Success and Women's Dress for Success -- which you can find in just about any bookstore. I have found, however, that there are a few special rules for lawyers who are interviewing with other lawyers, and they deserve special mention here.

1.   Dressing for Success in the Legal Job Interview

The key word here is "dull". Dull, dull, dull! The slightest hint of glitz, glamour, high fashion or sexiness will usually be enough to turn a lawyer-interviewer right off. Remember that one of your goals is to appear "low-key" and understated during a legal job interview. Similarly, your look should be "low-key" and muted in both color and style. For both men and women, the preferred color scheme is the same: navy blue or charcoal grey suit, a white shirt or blouse, and a maroon tie (either a solid maroon or a "club" tie with small -- very small -- repetitive designs on it). While it is certainly true that different regions of the United States have different customs when it comes to business dress (California is more casual, for example, than the Northeast), you cannot go wrong with a conservative, buttoned-down look that says "I am a professional; I take my work seriously." When in doubt, tone it down and take no chances; remember that your goal is not to knock the interviewer's socks off with your highly developed ability to co-ordinate colors, but rather to avoid making a negative impression. Your clothing should be a neutral factor in the decision made about your fit for the job; ideally the interviewer should not even notice what you are wearing.

Regarding perfumes and after shaves, the best smell in a legal job interview is no smell at all. Jewelry should be muted or nonexistent (except of course for wedding or engagement rings, as they indicate a certain stability in one's personal life).

What about a briefcase or other accessory? There is one school of thought that carrying a briefcase into an interview is a good idea, as it gives the interviewer an idea of how you will look when you walk into the firm (or company) each day. I personally do not subscribe to this theory; an interviewer knows that you do not walk around all day carrying a briefcase, and may suspect you are "brown nosing" him.

I normally do not carry anything with me during an interview; I leave my briefcase in the closet by the reception area, along with my topcoat, rubbers and umbrella (if it is raining). If the interviewer wants to see what I look like on the subway, he is welcome to escort me out of the office in person and watch while I put these things on.

I do, however, keep a spare copy of my resume in my suit jacket pocket; many times the interviewer will not have this handy on his desk (or it will be buried beneath his many piles of paperwork), and it makes you look organized if you can spare him the indignity of tearing through the mess on his desk before you can begin the interview (incidentally, it also prevents you from rehashing your resume verbally while the interviewer takes notes -- an awkward, undesirable and risky venture, because you want to be past the point where your credentials are being closely scrutinized).

2.   *Your Physical Appearance*

First impressions are everything, and social psychologists tell us that (sadly) first impressions are almost always the result of our reaction to a person's physical appearance. To put it simply, we are more likely to think good things about people we find personally attractive than about people we find personally repulsive.

It goes without saying that your body should be clean (I shower twice a day), your shirt and suit clean and pressed, your tie stainless, your hair clean and brushed in a conservative style (no spikes or ponytails). But your efforts should go beyond this; if your face is inclined to moles, you should have them removed if the cost is reasonable (but not right before the interview; ugly scars will make it hard for the interviewer to look at you straight on). If your teeth are crooked, you should visit an orthodontist about having them straightened. If your face bears the ravaging scars of acute acne, you should consider having your face "sanded" or some other minor cosmetic surgery performed. If your eyeglass frames do not "fit" your face it will look ludicrous (some people can wear tortoise shell hornrims, while others look better in aviator rims); visit an optometrist and get yourself fitted for contacts or an aesthetically more attractive frame.

A dark tan is definitely not a good idea, as it signals that you have a healthy, vibrant personal life outside of work which lawyers don't have -- at best they will think that you are not committed to the law, at worst they will be jealous of your lifestyle. A slight "lawyer's pallor" or paleness in the face is actually an asset in a legal job interview; it signals you are hardworking and able to stand up to the long hours that young lawyers must spend while they are apprenticing at their craft. Which brings us to beards and other forms of facial hair: sometimes facial hair is acceptable, but most of the time it is not. It is a prejudice of the lawyer's life that his appearance must not turn off clients, and there are quite a few clients (at least in the business world) who think that beards and moustaches should be worn only by college professors and anarchists. Again, the emphasis is not on personal style or popular taste; I personally happen to like beards, and sported a moustache in my youth.

Only you can judge if your prospective employer is flexible enough to "let you be yourself" while on the job; generally lawyers are much more tolerant of people's eccentricities than are other professionals (in most large corporations, for example, beards are absolutely taboo). I have found, however, that long term success in the legal profession often means carrying yourself in such a way that you alienate the fewest possible number of people; few people will dislike you because you don't have facial hair, while a considerable number will dislike you because you do. The decision is yours and yours alone, but if your grades are not top-notch, or you do not have enough portable business to sustain yourself, I suggest you err on the side of conformity for a while before you decide to set yourself apart from the madding crowd.

3.   *Habits and Body Language*

Idiosyncrasies do not sit well with interviewers generally. If you have any tics or habits, such as biting your nails or fidgeting, you must learn to control these before entering the interview room. One good way to control your hands is to practice three standard positions -- arms resting on your chair's arms with your hands holding onto (but not gripping for dear life) the ends of the armrests, hands folded in front of you, one arm resting on the chair's arm while the other hand is resting on the opposite knee (for example, if your left arm is resting on the chair's armrest, your right hand should be on your right knee in a relaxed position) -- and shift from one to the other periodically during the interview.

Note that psychologists tell us it is bad body language to cross your arms in front of you; such a position is essentially defensive, and signals suspicion or distrust of what is being said. Accordingly, this is a position you should avoid during an interview -- do not fold your arms across your chest, for example, and do not wrap one arm around your waist while the other rests on the chair's armrest. Similarly, you should always face the interviewer head on, and not turn your left or right side towards him at any point.

4.   How to Sit and Where to Sit

Your feet should remain firmly on the floor (no nervous tapping) and your posture should be roughly 90 degrees from the floor (no slouching over or leaning back in your chair). A common interviewing strategy is to offer you a plush chair or sofa, while the interviewer retains a straight-backed chair; if you are like me you will inevitably find yourself sinking lower and lower into the cushy chair's upholstery, such that the interviewer will be looking down at you throughout the interview. If given the choice you should always sit in a straight-backed chair.

Some interviewing offices are set up in such a way that you and the interviewer have two seating options: you either will sit on one side of the interviewer's desk while the interviewer sits on the other, or there will be an arrangement of chairs and sofas that will create for awkward moments as each of you figure out where to sit. In the latter case my preference is to let the interviewer sit down first, and then pick a chair or sofa as close to the interviewer as possible in which I am facing ninety degrees away from the interviewer (in other words, I am not looking him straight on, nor are we facing the same direction).

I find that this sends the desired warm signal that I am one of "his kind of people" (because we are not at odds with each other) while at the same time respecting the necessary formality of an interview situation (we are not sitting "on the same side of the table", at least not yet). If there is more than one interviewer, I make sure that my back is not turned to anyone, and that I am facing all of the interviewers as straight on as possible (to avoid the "ping-pong" effect of turning this way and that as questions are asked). If the interviewers position themselves such that this is not possible, I usually determine which of the interviewers has the most "clout" and position myself in the strongest position relative to him. For example, if I am being interviewed by a partner and an associate, and the two position themselves opposite each other, I will sit in between them but with the chair moved to the partner's side so that the associate can look at me and the partner as if we were equals. I will be at my preferred ninety-degree angle to the partner, while the partner will not be tempted to compare me with the associate as would be the case if the associate and I sat closely together.

Another example: if the partner and associate were to sit directly next to each other in what I call the "united front" formation, rather than sit directly across from them I would choose instead to sit at a ninety degree angle to the partner, on the opposite side of the partner from the associate (this usually forces the associate to adjust his position so as to break up the "united front", since otherwise he cannot look at me straight on).

Now, you may think that some of this game of "musical chairs" is simply silly. You are, after all, being reviewed on the strength of your credentials and perceived "fit" for the job, right? What does it matter where you sit, for crying out loud? Rather than disagree with you (frankly, much of this sort of thing is quite silly), I would simply point out that in many delicate international negotiations, in which war and peace may be at stake, the delegates (or their representatives) normally spend a great deal of time in determining the seating order. Obviously they consider it important that adversaries not be perceived by the press or public as friends or allies, and vice versa. They consider it important; why shouldn't you? The competition for legal positions is fierce these days, and you cannot afford to be "screened out" because of a silly thing having nothing whatever to do with what really counts: how good a lawyer you are (or have the promise of becoming).

5.   Eye Contact

How much eye contact should you maintain with the interviewer? Generally, you should position yourself so that your face is always in the interviewer's plain view, facing him straight on. You should maintain eye contact as much as possible, especially when you are answering one of the interviewer's questions, as this is viewed as a sign of sincerity and openness. However, you should not stare at him too closely, or follow his glance wherever it may roam. At best, this will make the interviewer uncomfortable; at worst (and especially if the two of you are of opposite sexes), it may be misread as taking a more personal interest in the interviewer than you might intend!

On the other hand, your eyes should not "wander"; a good solution is to allow your eyes to focus on points that are generally in the area of the interviewer's head, but without turning your head or otherwise appear to be looking away from the interviewer.

This problem of eye contact becomes especially acute when there are multiple interviewers. On the one hand, you don't want to appear to be playing to one interviewer at the expense of another (you don't, after all, really know who has the more clout); on the other hand, you don't want to seem like the spectator at a tennis or ping-pong match whose head moves perpetually back and forth while following the bouncing ball.

A good way to avoid this, as mentioned earlier, is to position your chair so that you are not caught directly between interviewers, and can look in the general direction of both (or all) while allowing your glance to move to the person who is speaking at that moment. Another good way to strike the right balance (especially if you are "caught in the middle" of a ping-pong situation) is to look at the person who is talking and, if the other asks a question, tilt your head in the direction of the person speaking while looking at a point equidistant between the two interviewers; by doing this you appear to be thinking about your answer in a way that does not make either inter- viewer think you are ignoring him.

D.   *The Key Rule For Success In A Legal Job Interview*

More than any other rule in this book, there is one rule you must keep foremost in your mind during a legal job interview. It is the key to success; disobeying or flaunting this rule is, in my opinion, the single biggest cause of being "screened out" in a legal job interview. It is a simple rule to remember, and yet is difficult to apply in practice, both because it runs counter to a lawyer's nature, and because it contradicts the advice given in countless books on interviewing (which, you will recall, are devoted to the professional interviewer or human resources executive, not the lawyer interviewer). It takes a lot of guts to follow this rule, but I guarantee that your interviewing performance will improve dramatically if you discipline yourself to follow it rigorously.

So what is this miracle rule? I can state it many ways, but it all boils down to five simple words:

SAY AS LITTLE AS POSSIBLE

That's it! That's all there is to it! The rule that, more than any other, will help you get ahead in the legal job interview.

SAY AS LITTLE AS POSSIBLE

As my Italian-American grandmother used to say, "Keep-a you bigga mouth shut, so you don't getta no flies in there!" Or, as my high school history teacher used to say, "in writing your essays for the final exam, be sure to keep them short, because the more you say, the more likely you are to make a mistake."

SAY AS LITTLE AS POSSIBLE

I call this the "20/80 Rule": I do not consider any legal job
interview a success if, upon reflection, I conclude that I have
done more than 20 percent of the total talking, and the interviewer has done less than 80 percent of the total talking (in
other words, we weren't just sitting there staring at each other
in stony silence).

Do you remember, from Chapter 1, the story of my two
interviews with Firm A and Firm B? Do you recall that I
thought I did wonderfully at Firm A, when in fact I was setting
myself up for a quick rejection? Do you recall that I thought I
did terribly during my afternoon of interviews at Firm B, and
ended up getting an offer from the head of the firm? Did you
wonder why that happened?

Well, now you know why! Because at Firm A I held
court like the Czar of All Russia; I chattered my head off at
each interview, selling and selling and selling my credentials
and experience, and hardly let the interviewers get a word in
edgewise. They probably thought I was such an egotistical jerk
that I deserved to be rejected from society at large, not merely
their firm! By contrast, at Firm B I let the interviewers do all of
the talking, for the simple reason that I was not adequately prepared for these interviews and didn't want to let it show.

The lawyers at Firm B probably thought I was fascinated by their war stories and perspectives on the practice of
law, which flattered them no end and led them to believe not
only that I was an incredible conversationalist, but had tremen-
dously sound judgment to boot! They probably thought they
had to rush to make me an offer or else I would be gobbled up
by more than one of their competing firms! Why?

BECAUSE I SAID AS LITTLE AS POSSIBLE

Most of the books on interviewing stress that, if an interview is handled correctly by the interviewer, the candidate will do the lion's share of the talking. That way he gets to open up and show the interviewer what he is really all about, so that the interviewer can make in-depth judgments about the candidate's poise, character, judgment, commitment, and above all "fit".

Which is all well and good, because these books are all about interviewing with professional interviewers: personnel people and human resources executives who have been intensely trained in the art of interviewing and know how to do it well. In contrast, in a legal job interview you are being interviewed by a lawyer who has not been so trained; by following the guidance of the interviewing books and doing all of the talking you are likely to make a bloody fool of yourself! Why?

Well, there are at least two reasons. First, by doing the lion's share of the talking you increase dramatically the odds that you might say something silly or counter to your self-interest, and thereby "screen yourself out" of the interviewing process. How can one little mistake or "slip of the tongue" screen you out? Let's make believe that you and I meet at a street corner, and that we discuss 10 topics. Let's further suppose that we agree warmly on nine of these topics, but we disagree strongly about the tenth. Then let's say we part company, and meet again at that same street corner a year later after not having seen each other at all during the interim. We may or may not, at that later time, remember any of the topics we agreed about during our earlier discussion, but we are sure to remember the tenth, which we disagreed about!

As a short digression, I submit that this is the reason that politicians are so noncommital in their statements about what they will do once they are elected to office, and fail to take strong stands on the issues. If I am running for office and you agree generally with my views on defense spending, the savings-and-loan crisis, aid to the homeless and the need for lower taxes, but you disagree violently with my views on abortion, tell me, what are you going to be thinking about when you pull the curtain behind you in that voting booth? If you are like most people, all you will think when you see my name underneath the voting lever is "that idiot Ennico, he's in favor of [either killing babies, or denying women their right to choose]!" and you will pass me over in favor of another candidate. As my father used to tell me when I was a boy, "better to keep your mouth shut and let people think you are a fool, than to open your mouth and prove it!"

There is no need to apologize for this; it is simply human nature, and until we can improve upon it, we must learn to live with it. A legal job interviewer, when he reflects upon the many candidates he has seen during his recent visit to XYZ Law School, or reviews the many resumes sitting on his desk after having been distracted by a client's business for the past week or two, will likely remember very few details about the candidate: what he looked like, what they talked about, what his grades were, whether he was a member of Law Review, and so forth (although you hope the interviewer would at least have made some notes on your resume during the interview).

He will, however, remember anything you said that sounded wrong or off-key to him, or that signaled a less-than-perfect fit with the position or the firm. So, simply put, the less you say, the less likely you are to say something bad or silly that the interviewer will remember. He will then be forced to make his decision based on what is on the piece of paper in front of him, which usually will be skewed in your favor (you wouldn't dare say anything negative about yourself in your resume, would you?)

The other important reason why talking a lot can "screen you out" in a legal job interview is much more cynical, and has more to do with how the interviewer sees himself than with how you present yourself during the interview. People in general like to hear nothing as much as the sounds of their own voices; no less an authority than Dale Carnegie, in his classic book _How To Win Friends And Influence People_ written almost a century ago, stressed the need to make other people feel important by really listening to what they have to say and not burdening them with the sound of your voice.

Now, in the legal job interview your interviewer is a lawyer, and lawyers more than most members of the human race like to be listened to. To put it crudely, a lawyer's job is to talk, and a lawyer loves nothing so much as to hear himself talk. The more you talk, the less interested in you the lawyer interviewer becomes. Why? Because, in the final analysis, the lawyer interviewer is more interested in himself and his own problems than he is interested in you and your career future. The more interest you show in the interviewer and his affairs, the more interested he will be in you. He will most likely perceive you as "his kind of person", and will remember you fondly as "the person who showed such a keen interest in my stamp collection (or my big case against the local electric utility)."

At the very least, he will not be able to say anything bad about you, because he was so busy talking that he neglected to ask you any questions about your background, experience, strengths and weaknesses! I have to believe that at some point in the process of selecting someone for a new position, all of the people who have interviewed the available candidates sit down around a table and compare the merits and attributes of each candidate. Very often in such situations the winner is not the person with the most impressive credentials, nor the person whose achievements make him stand head and shoulders over all the rest, but rather the person about whom the interviewers can say the fewest negative things.

You will recall from Chapter 2 that lawyers by nature are not risk takers; they tend to shoot for the safest and least risky course -- the easy single instead of the long-odds home run. This is no criticism of lawyers; they are paid by their clients not to take risks! How would you feel about your tax lawyer if he told you, "if you take this course of action, you stand a 99 percent chance of being audited by the I.R.S. But why don't you go ahead anyway? I think it's time we had a test case on this issue"? Something tells me you would not praise him for his innovative thinking and willingness to take risks (with your money, after all).

The surest way to put someone's mind at ease, and to win him over as a friend and ally, is to show a genuine and sincere interest in the things that matter most to him, which will usually not include your need to find a job, your need to become partner at his firm, or your need to advance your career. The best way to do this is to signal that you are willing to do things "his way" instead of yours -- that you are flexible, even malleable, and will easily adapt to whatever habits, style or culture your potential employer may want from its employees.

By asserting or "selling" yourself too strongly -- by talking too much -- you send an inaudible, but clear, signal to the interviewer that you are more interested in doing things your way, and there are few better ways to lose status in any organization than to let them think that you are a loner, some-one who "does his own thing", someone who does not do things "the company way," someone who is not a "team player," someone who "dares to be different," or someone who is not flexible in his attitudes and behavior on the job. Conversely, by saying little during an interview, you demon-strate that you are a good listener who is willing to do things the "right" way -- meaning, of course, the interviewer's way (or the way most befitting the employer's culture) -- and take the time to find out what that "right" way is before shooting your big mouth off or taking precipitous action.

What should you say during an interview? Obviously, if the interviewer asks you a direct question, you must answer it -- I am not counseling that you be evasive. Answer the question in the most direct, concise and short (short, short, short) manner possible, giving your answer the most positive "spin" you can. Once you have done so, then you should either shut up or (preferably) ask the interviewer a question.

Think of the legal job interview as a verbal tennis match -- like many of the great tennis players, your strategy is to keep the other player running back and forth, back and forth, from one side of the court to the other, so intent on returning your perfectly placed volleys that he forgets to go back on the offen-sive. Your volleys are your questions that you have carefully prepared in advance and committed to memory, after having thoroughly research the employer and the interviewer as recommended in Chapter 3. Whenever you find yourself in an awkward silence during a legal job interview, the solution is for you to ask the interviewer a question, not volunteer more information on something you may have already beaten to death. Keep the interviewer talking about himself, his practice, his great victory over the local electric utility, his great defense of the serial killer, his hobbies and personal interests, whatever! But keep him talking!

While you are keeping the interviewer talking, don't forget to listen to what he is saying! Your goal here is not to kill time, but to make the interviewer open up and babble on so much that he accidentally leaks some information about the employer and its practice that may actually be useful to you. If the interviewer confides that he is so busy that he has little or no time for outside interests, that will tell you more about the employer and its culture than a hundred page Martindale Hubbell entry ever will. While the interviewer is talking, you should be listening, not thinking about the next question to ask; if you listen carefully and closely enough, so closely that you actually lose track of time and space, the next question will suggest itself to you without any effort on your part.

If you can't think of a follow up question, you will pick out another of your memorized list of questions and ask it as soon as the interviewer finishes answering this one (if indeed he ever does).

A corollary of this basic rule should be mentioned in passing: "if the interviewer is selling you, shut up." If you sense during the interview that the interviewer is going out of his way to sell you on his employer or his practice, and especially if he is doing so openly, congratulations! You've got it made! He wants you and he is letting you know you have sold him on your credentials, your experience, and your personality. There is nothing more for you to do! So don't blow it by opening your mouth, getting carried away with your success, and blurting something out that is going to turn the interviewer around or make him doubt his judgment.

It bears repeating, that the key to success in the legal job interview -- the secret that more than any other will give you an edge over your competition -- is to

SAY AS LITTLE AS POSSIBLE

E.   _The Importance Of Being "Laid Back"_

1.   _Don't Sell_

In several places in this book, I have alluded to the importance of not "coming on too strong" during a legal job interview. The point needs to be underscored here, because your demeanor during the interview may be crucial to the outcome. While you should appear genuinely interested in the position and in the interviewer, you must not be too enthusiastic, or too dynamic, or too polished, or too eloquent, or else you risk screening yourself out as a viable candidate for the job. In a legal job interview, it actually helps to come across a bit on the dull, blase, uninteresting side.

This may at first appear contrary to common sense; aren't you supposed to make an effort to impress the interviewer, as all of the interview books recommend? Aren't you supposed to demonstrate that you stand head and shoulders above all the other candidates for the job? Aren't you supposed to "sell yourself"?

Strangely enough, in the legal job interview, the answer is a clear and resounding "no". It is precisely this sort of "salesmanship" that, you will recall, cost me my job offer from Firm A. I blew that interview because I came on too strong, and overpowered my lawyer interviewers, which had the effect of turning them right off.

Why is this so? Why is it necessary to come across a bit on the dull side to impress a legal job interviewer? Well, first let's take a look at the lawyer interviewer. He is first and foremost a lawyer, not a professional interviewer. And lawyers are notoriously resistant to sales pitches of all types and forms: there is nothing -- I mean nothing -- that the average lawyer detests more than Madison Avenue hype and a slick sales presentation. While the ability to "sell, sell, sell" may be an asset in the business world, it is an absolute liability in a legal job interview.

This is not to say that lawyers cannot be persuaded to buy something; it means only that they must sell themselves -- you cannot by your own action close the sale. The lawyer interviewer will want to weigh carefully the pros and cons of your background and experience, assess in his own mind your perceived "fit" with his employer, and come to a reasoned and balanced conclusion, much as he would in analyzing a client's legal problem.

2.   *Show That You Are Adaptable*

An even more important, albeit cynical, reason why you should not appear to be "selling" the interviewer is the interviewer's desire to hire someone who is cut from his own image. Ultimately, the person who will be hired for any legal position will be the candidate who the decisionmakers feel most closely conform to their stereotype of the successful lawyer in their particular environment. The decisionmakers must feel, in their collective gut, that you either behave the way they believe someone in your new position should behave, or that you have the capacity to adapt and conform your behavior to fit the style and culture of the organization. If the decision-makers cannot comfort themselves that you are a "blank slate" upon which the organization can write whatever it wishes -- if the decisionmakers believe you are too set in your ways and have too strong opinions on certain matters -- they are likely to conclude that you are too risky to take on board, and you will be screened out.

This is a sad but true aspect of organizational life: to succeed often means suppressing one's natural desires and opinions and tempering one's eagerness, enthusiasm and personal dynamism. In the words of an old Chinese proverb, "the nail that sticks up from the rest is the one that will be hammered down." This is, one suspects, what is actually meant when someone says that they want a "team player" -- they want someone who follows orders well, does his job in coordi-nation with others, and wears the team uniform, not someone who follows his own agenda. If you signal to the interviewer that you are too much of an individual, or that you are not willing to take the time to learn the "right" way of doing things (translation: the way the powerful people within the organiza-tion believe is the right way to do things), it will be an auto-matic screen out.

3.   *Conceal Your Dynamism*

Aside from concerns about "team playership", it is worth observing that many lawyers are fairly dull themselves -- their long hours and near total commitment to their work often prevent them from having many outside interests, and they are not the sort of people who liven up a cocktail party. Most lawyers would admit this is perhaps the most serious drawback of the legal profession. As such, they may well feel threatened by someone who is obviously more cultured, better read, and more interesting than they are.

In the extreme case, the lawyer interviewer who perceives himself as undynamic will be concerned that you may try to seduce his clients away from him, and will be jealous of your superior social skills. When dealing with such an interviewer it is best to make him think that you are even duller than he is, that you are absolutely no threat to him, and that your goal in life (just like his) is to make sure the job gets done right and the client is happy.

Thus, the way to carry yourself during a legal job interview is what I call "laid back": your facial expression should be relaxed and not too expressive; your speech should be low in volume and pitch, and should avoid strong inflections (a cultivated monotone -- what one lawyer friend of mine calls the "lawyer's whisper" -- is desirable here); your posture should not convey an image of intensity; your walk should be slow and deliberate, like a cat treading carefully to avoid alerting his prey; and your dress should be understated and perhaps even a little dull.

What is most important is that you not appear to be too dynamic or interesting. You should avoid discussing interests outside the law to the extent possible.

4.   _Never Opine On Anything_

Finally, you should avoid expressing your opinion on any subject whatsoever unless the interviewer invites you to do so (and even then I would try to fudge it). This is true even if the subject of your opinion seems relatively harmless.

A friend of mine once blew a legal job interview with a small firm in a suburban town when the interviewer asked how he felt about smaller firms in general. As part of my friend's answer -- to buttress his point that it was often difficult to maintain a collegial, friendly working atmosphere in a large law firm -- he inadvertently expressed the opinion that it is difficult for a law firm to operate in a collegial manner once there are more than 50 attorneys in the firm.

My friend of course had done his homework, and knew that the firm had significantly less than that number. Well, as it turns out my friend's interviewer was an ambitious sort whose goal was to see the firm grow to 100 lawyers; my friend's opinion was the last thing he wanted to hear, as it signaled that he would be a continuing dissenter from the interviewer's dreams of empire once hired. The interview ended abruptly at that point; my friend had said the thing the interviewer needed to hear in order to screen him out.

You never can know in advance what your interviewer thinks about any subject, so why risk disagreeing with him? Nine times out of ten you can avoid expressing opinions at all

during a legal job interview, and even in the tenth situation --
when your opinion on a matter is expressly invited by the
interviewer -- you can hedge your bets by saying something
like "well, I don't really have any strong opinion on the subject,
but I have heard others say [or "I have read"] that thus-and-
such is usually the case. I'm curious, what are your views on
the subject?"

Far from making you appear wishy washy, this type of
answer will signal to the interviewer that you don't jump to
conclusions without knowing what the other person is looking
to hear and without knowing the depth of the other person's
convictions. That is an extremely positive attribute in a legal
counselor, who cannot risk offending a client at any cost.

To summarize: to succeed in a legal job interview you
must not sell yourself in a direct manner, you must demonstrate
that your behavior is adaptable to your work environment, you
must never appear to be interesting or dynamic, and you must
never express an opinion on any subject unless you are dead
certain that the interviewer agrees with your views.

F.   Asking The Right Questions

The key to saying as little as possible is to keep the
interviewer talking as much as possible, and the key to doing
that is to keep asking questions. But not just any questions; to
keep the interviewer talking, and genuinely interested in the
one-way discussion, your questions must be the "right" ones.
We will discuss in this section how to go about asking the
"right" questions; Chapter 7 will discuss some strategies for
answering some commonly asked interviewer questions in the
"right" way.

The "right" question in a legal job interview has three characteristics: (1) it must be pertinent to your twin goals of getting the interviewer on your side and establishing your perfect "fit" for the job; (2) it must not be too direct for fear of turning the interviewer off; and (3) it must put you in the best possible light.

1.   *The Question Must Help You Achieve Your Goals*

What do we mean when we say the question must be "pertinent to your twin goals of getting the interviewer on your side and establishing your perfect 'fit' for the job?" Simply that: in asking a question you are seeking either to impress the interviewer with the depth of your research or your shared experience, or you are seeking information you can use to show the interviewer how perfect you would be for the job. If a question does not serve either (or both) of these goals, it should not be asked.

You may be intently curious about weather conditions in the city where the interviewer's firm is located, but if you ask "tell me, Mr. So-and-So, what was it doing in XYZ City when you left this morning?", the interviewer cannot help but wonder where you are heading (most lawyers I know do not have much patience with small talk). A better way to satisfy your curiosity is to watch The Weather Channel on cable television, or consult the newspaper "USA Today".

2.   *The Question Must Not Be Too Direct*

What about the second characteristic of a good interview question -- that it not be so direct that it turns the interviewer off? Simply that: while there is certain information about the employer's style and culture you simply must know in order to make an intelligent career decision, there are some things you cannot find out about by asking a direct question. For example, if you were to ask the interviewer "tell me, is your firm a sweatshop?", the interviewer would think you a total clod, (1) because any firm in which he is a partner is definitely not a sweatshop, and (2) because you have just sent him a signal that you are not willing to work hard to learn your profession.

A better way to obtain the information you want, without risking a turnoff, is to ask indirect questions designed to elicit statistical information, such as: "are there any expectations as to the number of hours a first year associate is expected to work at your firm?"; "are you satisfied with the amount of personal time you and your colleagues have at this point in your lives?"; and "are you satisfied with the amount of associate turnover your firm has experienced in the past few years?"

Similarly, you should avoid questions about the firm's weaknesses and "sore points", even if you think you can phrase them in a positive manner. Questions such as "tell me, how is your firm handling that massive legal malpractice judgment that was rendered against you last year?" or "tell me, is it true what I read in last week's Fortune magazine that your company is planning on a major downsizing of staff later this year?" are guaranteed to make the interviewer feel ill at ease and question your judgment in being so direct.

Better ways to handle these questions are to phrase them as follows: "tell me, how does your firm handle quality control as a general matter? Is there much close supervision of

associates in the early years?" and "tell me, what is your
company's overall strategy for adding or reducing legal staff this
year?" Note that these phrasings of the same question are
more general and value neutral, and give the interviewer more
latitude in putting a positive "spin" on the answer. Just be sure
to listen to the answers closely, and listen for the "music", not
just the words.

3.   The Question Must Make You Look Good

Finally, you must keep in mind that by asking questions
you are interested not only in eliciting information from the
interviewer; you are trying to impress the interviewer with your
intelligence, tact and judgment. If a question does not make
you look good, there is no point in asking it.

What sorts of questions will make you look good?
Generally, there are two kinds: questions that play to the
interviewer's "hot buttons" (such as a special interest or current
problem -- something the interviewer could talk about for
hours); and good questions that the other 25 candidates have
not thought to ask. An example of the former is "Mr. So-and-
So, I see that you chair the state bar association's Blue Sky Law
Committee; tell me, what do you think of the current proposal
in Congress to develop uniform standards for state 'blue sky'
laws?" An example of the latter is "Mr. So-and-So, I see that
your company is affiliated with a French financial institution
with substantial interests in the Middle East; tell me, will your
company be involved at all in helping Kuwait get back on its
feet again?"

The answers to these questions may, of course, be
irrelevant to the position you are applying for; their purpose,

however, is to show the interviewer you have done your homework and are thinking about the same sorts of things that keep him awake at night. At the very least, he will know that you don't ask the same questions of every interviewer.

4.   *Some Good Interview Questions*

The key to asking good questions is to do your research as recommended in Chapter 3, ask yourself if each question satisfies all three characteristics of a "good" interview question, and then memorize the question so that you can introduce it naturally and gracefully during the interview. With the under-standing that there are no good "form questions" for a legal job interview, here are some good interview questions that I believe fit all three categories. You should feel free (and indeed must) conform them to your own style of speaking and your own interests.

If I were to start working in this position today, what sorts of projects would I be working on? I find this is a better question than "what sorts of skills are needed for this position?" because it focuses the interviewer on the tasks he needs done right now, and gives you a much more detailed sense of the level of responsibility and client contact you can expect from the position. By asking follow up questions about specific transactions, research projects, or cases, you can get quite a bit of mileage out of this one.

When you think about your practice and where it's going, what sorts of things are you happiest about? Note that this question parallels that favorite of legal job interviewers: "what do you consider your strengths?" or "what is your greatest strength?" By asking this question you have simply turned the table on the interviewer, in what I believe is a fair and nonthreatening way. By getting the interviewer to open up about his own personal feelings about the practice of law in general (and the practice at his current employer), you can learn a great deal about how you will probably feel once you have reached the interviewer's level. You also send a signal to the interviewer, without saying so, that you are seriously considering being someday in his shoes, which any interviewer will find flattering. Note that you should avoid asking the converse of this question -- "when you think about your practice and where it's going, what are you most worried about?" -- because it focuses the interviewer on a negative which will inevitably be transferred to you. A better way to ask this question, if you absolutely must, is "do you have any concerns at the moment about where your practice is going?"

Is There A Specialty You Don't Currently Have In-House That You Would Like To Develop In-House? This question has two purposes. The first is to get a sense of the employer's goals and weaknesses (or perhaps a sense of how their clients' businesses are faring; a sudden interest in bankruptcy work could spell trouble for the employer in the long run), and to learn about that part of the employer's practice that is most likely to experience growth over the next few years. The second purpose is a bit more insidious: you are sending the lawyer interviewer two very positive signals -- that you are a market driven attorney who is willing to adapt his skills to his clients' changing needs, and that you are interested in becoming one of the young attorneys who help the employer develop and grow into the desired area of practice. With a little bit of research, you may be able to answer this question yourself before the interview begins, and thus be ready to follow this question up with a brief summary of the work you have done in the desired area.

If you had to narrow it down to one thing, what do you think is the key to success in this position (or, for an entry level position, "the key to success to getting ahead in your organization")? The interviewer's answer to this question will tell you a great deal about the employer's culture and its image of itself. Don't expect to hear the truth, but listen closely anyway; if the interviewer stresses "the ability to get along well with people", you know that politics are very important to getting ahead. If on the other hand the interviewer emphasizes "the ability to work hard and get the job done", you know the place is a sweatshop where there will be little or no time for politics.

These are very general questions, and will need to be supplemented by a lengthy list of job-specific and employer-specific questions that you will generate in the course of your research. Some "generic" questions are listed below, with the warning that rarely if ever should they asked in precisely this form; should you do so you risk appearing "packaged" and this will turn the lawyer interviewer off. You should feel free, however, to tailor these questions to the circumstances of the particular employer and interviewer, as they are designed to elicit extremely important information.

Questions For Law Firm Positions

What is the firm's client base and how (if at all) has it changed over the past ten years? What changes in the client base do you foresee in the future?

What areas of practice is the firm most known for? Is it a "boutique" firm with only a handful of specialties, or does it have a more diverse range of specialties in-house? What is the culture associated with the specialty (generally, bankruptcy work is considered to require a more aggressive temperament, while trusts and estates work is considered to require a more genteel and comforting disposition)?

What is the turnover rate for associates after the first three years? The first five? In each of the past five years, how many associates have been made partner as a rough percentage of the total number of associates who were considered for partnership positions (I find that this question generates more useful information than simply asking about the firm's partner to associate ratio, since the latter does not take into account changes in the firm's practice or client base)? Generally, where have those associates who have been passed over tend to find work once they leave the firm?

How important are business generating skills in determining whether an associate will be made a partner?

What does the firm do in terms of training associates in their assigned duties (for an entry level position, you are probably more concerned about the quality of the education you will receive there than with your prospects of making partner, which is a long way in the future)? If the firm needs to grow into new areas of practice, will they do so by retraining their associates or by hiring laterals from other firms (or merging with another firm that practices in the desired area)?

How are the partners and associates divided into "teams"? To how many partners and senior associates will an associate have to report on each team?

Do the partners of the firm generally get along well? Will the partners that head up a particular team be likely to agree on those matters that are most important to the associate, such as the quality of his work (reinforced by periodic reviews), his training and professional development, the number of desired billable hours, and the need for the associate to become involved in outside activities?

What is the firm's culture? Is it aggressive, polished, "white shoe", low key? Is there a tolerance for a diversity of associates in terms of race, gender, ethnicity and so forth? How tolerant is the firm of an individual's eccentricities? Does the firm have longstanding ties to a particular charity or political party?

Does the firm believe that public service or community legal work is important? Have any of the partners served in government or other nonlegal appointments? How important is the "bottom line" to the firm (it is always important, but is it the only thing that is important)?

Questions For Corporate Legal Positions

What is the key to success in winning the confidence of the businesspeople? Is the legal department highly or poorly regarded within the organization? Is inside counsel expected to "lead" the businesspeople, or is the inside counsel's role limited to counseling the businesspeople and letting them make the final decisions?

Who are the company's outside counsel (there will usually be more than one firm depending on the type of work involved), and how strong are the company's ties to each firm (i.e., if the general counsel came from Firm X, you can be sure Firm X will always get at least a certain amount of work from the company)? Is the company looking to change its relationships with outside counsel in any way? Are there any areas in which the company's businesspeople believe they are not being adequately served by existing outside counsel?

As between inside and outside counsel, who is expected to take the lead on transactions? Is inside counsel expected to attend every meeting and negotiating session? Is the inside counsel expected to "manage" the outside counsel's costs?

Is the position more of a "work" position (one in which the inside counsel's job is primarily to do the technical legal work on smaller matters, and the larger matters are handled by outside counsel with minimal involvement by the inside counsel) or a "managing" position (one in which the inside counsel is expected to know only a little about a lot of things and focus his energies instead on managing the company's relationships with outside counsel and participating in company business decisions)?

If the position is with a corporate subsidiary, how do the legal departments at the parent and subsidiary level interface? How much freedom of operation is allowed to the subsidiary's attorneys?

Questions For Government Agencies

What is the agency's mandate from Congress (or the state legislature), and how has it changed over the years (i.e., is the agency's authority expanding or shrinking)? Upon which aspects of the agency's mandate are the senior lawyers currently focusing their efforts (rarely are all of an agency's regulations enforced with equal zeal at all times)? Are there areas in the agency's mandate in which the senior lawyers feel more enforcement effort is needed?

Are lawyers at the agency expected to play a role in expanding or clarifying policy? For example, if the agency receives a request for an administrative ruling which evidences a "hole" in the agency's regulatory structure, how involved will the staff lawyer become in this process? Do staff lawyers ever become involved in the legislative committees that draft laws which affect the agency's mandate?

Whom does the agency regard as its primary constituents? Does it tend to cozy up to the people it regulates, or is it a "watchdog" that doesn't give an inch when interpreting its regulations and its mandate?

Does the current governmental administration have any expectations about how strong or lax an enforcement effort will be made by the agency? If it does, has it provided the agency with adequate support in achieving the administration's goal?

What is the average tenure in office of lawyers at the agency? Is there a "revolving door" by which lawyers seek jobs in the private sector after a few years at the agency? If so, where do they tend to go and why do they leave?

G.   *Handling The Interviewer's Questions*

Chapter 7 will give you some strategies for answering the most common interview questions, such as "what are your greatest strengths?" and "why are you leaving your current job?" (or, for an entry level position, "why did you decide to become a lawyer?") In this section I want only to highlight the point, made in earlier sections, that your answers must be direct and to the point, must be as short as is humanly possible, and must end either in your silence or in a question for the interviewer which may or may not be related to the question he asked you. Remember that your objective in a legal job interview is to keep the interviewer talking as much as possible; keep that ball in his court!

I use a fifteen second rule when answering an interviewer's question. I try to anticipate the interviewer's questions (and after a few interviews, this will become quite easy as the same questions tend to come up time and again; remember that lawyers as a rule are not very imaginative) and prepare in my mind a response that will take no more than fifteen seconds. If I find myself taking more than fifteen seconds to answer a particular question, I will stop and ask the interviewer "am I reading your question correctly?" This gets the interviewer talking again, if only for a brief moment, and gives me the chance to obtain a clearer focus on what he's driving at. When the ball returns to my court I make a very short reply and follow up with a question.

What do you do if the interviewer asks you a question and you really haven't the foggiest idea of what the answer should be? Most interviewing books will tell you you should buy a second or two by saying something like "that's an interesting question; I would have to think about that for a moment," and I heartily endorse that approach. But what if you still can't come up with an answer?

First, don't panic. The interviewer may not (and usually will not) be looking for an answer, but wants to know how you handle yourself in a difficult situation. If you try to fudge it, you will "screen yourself out" of the interviewing process; no lawyer likes to hear baloney from a client or a junior attorney. Rather than guess and guess wrong, my preferred approach is to try to find out where the interviewer is headed; I may say something like "that's an interesting question, and I'm frankly surprised it has never come up before. Tell me, what is it about my background or experience that you are especially concerned about (or that you are especially interested in knowing more about)?" Usually this will signal to the interviewer that I am slightly confused by his question, and he will take some pains to clarify his intentions; if I listen closely enough, I usually will be able to figure out what he is looking for and be able to give it to him.

What if this does not work? I keep trying to clarify the question. I may repeat it in a slightly different fashion, using words that bring it closer in form to a question I am prepared to answer, and ask the interviewer if that is what he means to ask (I am careful of course not to appear to be evading the question). Under no circumstances, however, will I guess at an answer. If all else fails, and I can't figure out where the interviewer is headed, I may say something like "you know, Mr. So-and-So, I really haven't given much thought to that; I guess I didn't think anyone would be all that interested in that. I'd like to think about your question a bit and give you an answer later in the day.

Will that be all right with you? I'd rather take the time to give you the right answer than blurt out something which won't be useful to you." Usually this will turn the interviewer to another topic and end the awkwardness (I will, by the way, always follow up on my promise to get back to him later in the day).

At best, I have satisfied his concern that I am not the sort of lawyer to "shoot from the hip" and answer difficult questions without doing the necessary homework. At worst, he will think that I am not sufficiently "fast on my feet" and screen me out, but at least I will now know another interview question for which I must have a ready answer. Incidentally, do you write down different or unusual questions that you are asked during job interviews? I do; in fact I keep a file of recurring questions and an outline of my preferred answer to each one. Why reinvent the wheel each time you go out into the job market-place?

There is one situation in particular in which you may find yourself at a loss for words -- when the interviewer asks you a technical question about an area of law or practice in which you are holding yourself out as having some expertise. Chapter 7 will give you some advice on handling that very delicate situation (which, by the way, does not commonly occur; most lawyer interviewers will take your resume at its word).

H.   Dealing With "Negative" Questions

Once in a while, especially if your lawyer interviewer is a litigator or trial attorney, you may find yourself the focus of a "negative" or "adversary" interview. This is one in which all of the interviewer's questions appear to be designed to put you down or make you reveal unflattering or negative information about yourself, and it can be a truly terrifying experience. Even in a normal job interview, you may encounter one or two questions in which the interviewer appears to be less than impressed with something in your background or experience.

If you should ever be subject to such an interview, or if such a question should arise, keep in mind that things are not usually as they seem. In most cases the interviewer doesn't really think you are a jerk, and isn't prejudiced against you before you walk into the room. Otherwise, why would he be taking the time to talk to you (remember that your mental attitude should be that you already have the job before you walk in the door).

In situations where the tone of the entire interview is negative, the interviewer's purpose is not to humiliate you (although if you are not careful he may well succeed; litigators are very good at cross examining people and tearing apart their prepared stories), but rather to see if you are tough enough to survive in what he believes is a rough practice, a difficult environment or an aggressive culture. In the situation where the overall tone of the interview is positive but the interviewer asks one or two negative questions, what is usually happening is that the interviewer has surfaced one or two things on your resume that he thinks he will have trouble selling to his partners or colleagues, and wants you to tell him what he should tell these people when they express their concern about these particular things.

Whatever you do in this situation, there are three important rules to keep in mind.

First, don't be defensive. By reacting to the question with surprise, shock or horror, you send a signal to the interviewer that you had something to hide and (shucks!) the interviewer has discovered the skeleton in your closet. Your first response to such a situation probably should be something like "I anticipated that you would ask me about that." This puts the interviewer at ease, and tells him that he probably won't have too difficult a job explaining this one difficult item. Also, be sure to keep your answer as short as possible. The more you make a big deal out of the negative item, the more the interviewer will too.

Second, remember that no one can intimidate you without your consent. You didn't go to law school because you wanted to be a shrinking violet. The legal profession is tough, combative, aggressive and downright dirty at times. Show the interviewer that you can take the pressure without losing your cool. Remain calm at all times but be sure to be assertive about your strengths, your achievements, and the positive aspects of your resume. In fact, if you sense that the interview is going to be entirely negative, you are free to ignore the interviewer's specific questions to a certain extent.

A simple example will illustrate the point. Let's say you know something about cars, and I sell you my old used car with a promise that it will get 30 miles to a gallon on the highway. You don't ask me about the state of the brakes, and I have no reason to tell you anything about the brakes because I don't notice anything wrong with them. Two weeks later you call me on the telephone and tell me the brakes on my old car are worn through and need to be replaced immediately.

Of course if I value your friendship I will make some accommodation. But if I don't know you from a hole in the wall, and if I have reason to believe you should have known what you were doing when you bought the car and should have had the brakes tested at that time, one perfectly valid response to your telephone call is for me to smile and ask "but tell me, are you getting 30 miles to the gallon on the highway?" In other words, just because a person has asked you a leading question does not mean you have to give him a direct answer; you can counter a negative with a positive.

Third, in answering an interviewer's question you never, ever, ever volunteer negative information about yourself. Even if the lawyer interviewer accuses you of having done something in your past that you know darn well is true, you never admit this to the interviewer unless you want to be "screened out" immediately. When this happens your preferred response is not to deny that it happened, but to explain it in a low key, off-the-cuff manner, in a way that any reasonable interviewer will find plausible, and then turning the interviewer's focus back on himself as quickly as possible (I have observed that people who like to engage in "adversary" interviews are also people who love to hear themselves talk).

If, for example, the interviewer asks "isn't it true, Mr. Candidate, that you have spent only an average of six months on each of your last three jobs?", it is much better to say something like "well, I'm sure you know this industry has had a rough time of it in the current recession; all three of my last employers went through substantial downsizings and when you're the last hired, you tend to be the first to be laid off -- isn't this your experience, Mr. So-and-So?" than to say "yes, you're right; I guess that makes me look like a job hopper or an incompetent, huh?" Appealing to an interviewer's sympathy and compassion is not usually a good strategy; most lawyers I know are not overly gifted with these emotions.

The best strategy when dealing with negative questions is to turn the question into a positive statement about yourself. If, for example, the lawyer interviewer were to ask you "I see from your data sheet, Mr. Candidate, that you have been divorced three times; not much of a family man, are you?" (incidentally, I think any interviewer who asked this question in such a blatant manner is opening himself and his employer up to a lawsuit, if not a punch in the mouth; I am using this example because it is clear, not because I think it is a real world question), you could say something like "well, Mr. So-and-So, my spouses haven't been too tolerant of my long hours at the office, it's true; it's really hard to find someone who really understands my commitment to the law and my total involvement in my work -- there really are days when I just lose track of the time, and I feel I can't let go of the problem until I am satisfied I have found the right answer -- tell me, how do you manage to reconcile career and family life in your demanding practice?" (note that by answering in this fashion, you may make the interviewer start to wonder if he is as committed to the law as he thinks he is). Not every situation, of course, lends itself to this approach, but if you can pull it off it is the legal job interviewing equivalent of the grand slam home run.

I.   _Handling The Awkward Silence_

It happens every once in a while; you have answered an interviewer's question, keeping your answer short, concise and to the point. You then wait for the interviewer to say something or ask the next question. But nothing happens. The interviewer simply nods his head and encourages you to go on, or just sits there like a statue and glares at you. Several awkward seconds pass, and you frantically start thinking of ways toresume the dialogue. You have reached an impasse; neither you nor the interviewer seem capable of getting the interview going again.

I have never fully figured out why this happens so often in legal job interviews, but awkward silences are part of the game you must learn to play. As best as I can figure, there are three possible reasons for an awkward silence, in decreasing order of likelihood: (1) the interviewer is playing a game with you to test your poise in dealing with an awkward situation -- he wants nothing more than to see you lose your cool so that he can "screen you out" as an unstable candidate who has not fully reached maturity; (2) the interviewer's people skills are not well developed and he simply does not know what to say either; or (3) the interviewer has fallen asleep with his eyes open (or, in one case that actually happened to a friend of mine, suffered a massive stroke and died) during your last answer.

Whatever the reason, there is a simple two-step strategy that will help you overcome the awkwardness and get the conversation going again in a way that makes you look like a seasoned professional.

Step One is to simply say nothing: look at the interviewer and wait for him to say something. Don't be afraid to let a few seconds pass in this fashion, as the awkwardness is mutual and the interviewer will be just as eager as you are to get things going again. What you don't want to do at any cost is to start babbling about anything and everything just to end the awkward silence. Remember the cardinal rule of legal job interviewing: **SAY AS LITTLE AS POSSIBLE**. You have already answered the interviewer's last question to your satisfaction (and probably to his as well); if he wants you to expand upon your answer, let him give you an idea of what he wants. Just stare at him for a few seconds.

Under no circumstances should you let an awkward silence last more than a few seconds; if you do you will appear to be nonverbal in the interviewer's eyes, and no lawyer ever wants to think of himself or another lawyer as nonverbal. If after a few seconds the silence remains unbroken, it is time to resort to Step Two: ask the interviewer one of your prepared questions. Don't worry that the question is unrelated to the previous topic of discussion; your goal here is to turn the initiative back where it belongs -- in the interviewer's hands -- and get him to start talking again. Most interviewers (especially in the second scenario described above where the interviewer is a slug and doesn't know what to talk about either) will be delighted or relieved at this approach, as it is exactly what a lawyer would do if a client "clammed up" on him during a counseling session.

If you sense that your interviewer has fallen asleep during the last answer, there is one sure way to find out: remain silent for a moment of two, and if there appear to be no signs of life in the interviewer, clear your throat sharply and loudly. If that does not produce a response, you may wish to say, in a fairly loud voice, "Mr. So-and-So, would you like me to expand at all on my previous answer?" If there is still no response, you should begin to suspect cardiac arrest; what my friend did in the awful episode described above was to leave the office, walk calmly up to the late interviewer's secretary, and say "excuse me, ma'am, but I believe there's something wrong with Mr. So-and-So; could you please have a look at him with me? I think he's passed out" (and no, I do not know whether or not my friend was offered the job).

J.   *Closing The Interview*

Just as the most hazardous parts of an airline flight are
the takeoff and the landing, so the most awkward parts of a
legal job interview are the beginning (where you are greeting
the interviewer and trying to establish a personal rapport with
him) and the end (where you are taking your leave and trying
to end the interview on a positive note). Here are some simple
ules to remember when a legal job interview comes to an end.

Rule Number One: let the interviewer decide when the
interview is over. If your interview is scheduled to last fifteen
or thirty minutes, remember that time schedules are not graven
by and reminds him of your schedule. Never be the one to
terminate the interview -- it sends a signal to the interviewer
that you really did not enjoy talking to him, and he will screen
you out.

Rule Number Two: express your enthusiasm for the job
and for the interviewer. A good closing statement, modified as
always to reflect your speaking habits, is "I've really enjoyed
meeting you, Mr. So-and-So; you have a wonderful practice
here at Dewey Cheatham & Howe and I would love to be a
part of it." This closes the interview on an upbeat note, com-
forts the interviewer that he has not said anything to turn you
off to the position, and sets you apart from those (and they are
many) who do a good job of interviewing but fail to tell the
interviewer that they want the job.

Rule Number Three: if the interviewer walks you on to
in stone: if the interviewer runs over his alloted time (and this
happens often), don't be fool enough to tell him so -- let him
ramble on with his interminable war story until the next inter

viewer (or more likely the legal personnel coordinator) comes your next interview appointment, or escorts you to the door at the end of the day, be sure to continue talking to him. The interview is formally over, but there is no rule that says you cannot continue asking pertinent questions or make small talk with the interviewer right up to the final handshake. Continuing the conversation in an informal way signals to the interviewer that you are really a decent individual, confirms that what the interviewer saw during the "formal" interview session is the way you are in real life, and underscores your enthusiasm for the position.

A word about handshakes. You probably already know that your handshake must be firm but not bone-crushing, and should not involve the sort of vigorous arm movement you would use in pumping a well. Keep in mind also that you should shake hands with the interviewer only twice: once at the very beginning of the interview, and once as you are going out the door. If the interviewer escorts you out of the employer's offices, a third handshake may also be in order, but use discretion; shaking hands too many times demonstrates insecurity and uncertainty about social protocol.

K.   Following Up

When do you send a follow-up letter after an interview, and when do you refrain from doing so? Generally, I send a thank-you note in one of three situations: (1) where the interviewer or the employer has gone out of his way to do me a kindness (such as fly me up to the firm's offices at the firm's expense, or give me an autographed copy of his latest lawbook); (2) where I am concerned that something I said during the interview may not be taken the right way and I wish to clarify my meaning before the interviewer has a chance to screen me out (this only if I am strongly interested in the position); and (3) where the interviewer and I have uncovered a special common interest and I wish to remind him of that common interest (once an interviewer and I discussed a common interest in a famous music group of the 1960s; the following Sunday I read an article in a local newspaper that one of the group's founders had died suddenly; I sent the interviewer a copy of the article together with a short handwritten note saying "don't know if you saw this -- I know you will feel as badly as I do").

Where you decide a note is appropriate, the note should be short (never longer than a page and usually not longer than two paragraphs), and should reiterate your enthusiasm for the position and the interviewer without being unctuous. If possible your note should also remind the interviewer of anything out of the ordinary that you discussed during the interview that will help the interviewer remember you in a positive light (in the case above, I might have said in my follow-up note "it was good to meet someone else who remembers fondly the XYZ Band from the 1960's").

Where the employer is paying certain of your interviewing expenses, it is best to keep the thank-you note separate from the "expense account" letter in which you seek reimbursement for those expenses; better still, send the thank-you note to the most important interviewer you met, and send the expense itemization to someone else at the employer -- someone less influential -- whose job it is to handle such things (like a law firm's recruitment coordinator).

CHAPTER 5

SOME SPECIAL RULES FOR
THE LUNCHEON INTERVIEW

A.   It Is Not Just A Social Occasion

At some point in your interviewing career it is inevitable
that you will be taken by your prospective employer to a fancy
restaurant for lunch, cocktails and/or dinner. The purpose of
such an interview is threefold: (1) to give all of the involved
parties a treat at the expense of the United States Treasury (and
hence indirectly from the United States taxpayer, namely you
and me); (2) to see how you handle yourself in a social situation
away from the office; and (3) to get you away from the office in
a relaxed setting so that you will be more likely to let your
guard down and say some stupid things that will help the
interviewers screen you out.

You will recall from Chapter 1 my interview with Firm
A, particularly the part where I was taken to a famous four-star
restaurant by a number of the firm's associates. If I had had the
benefit of this book when that luncheon interview took place, I
would have known a number of things that I did not then know.
First, I would have guessed that the associates were all member
of the Legal Personnel Committee and thus were not in a
position to "tell tales out of school" even if I hoped in my heart
of hearts that they would. Second, the fact that no partner was
present would have alerted me to be on my very best behavior,
as I was being led to believe that I could safely let my guard
down with a bunch of men and women who, after all, seemed
to be my peers in age and experience. Of course, in reality
nothing could have been further from the truth; the whole

purpose of this exercise was to put me in a position to let my guard down, and that's just what happened.

Finally, I should have been alert to the fact that a boon-doggle like this was just as exciting for the young associates (who probably had been slaving until after midnight each night for the preceding month) as it was for me, and would have known how to turn that to my advantage.

As it turned out, I did not have the benefit of this book. Instead I went like a lamb to the slaughter, let my hair down, talked incessantly, told every one of my awful war stories, drank way too much, and generally made a bloody fool of myself. As you know, the result was that I did not get an offer from Firm A, but the quickest rejection letter in recorded history (I think they even sent it certified mail to make sure I would get it promptly).

B.   Don't Relax

Lawyers like to think of themselves as social animals, and a large part of their success or failure as professionals depends on how well (or how poorly) their clients perceive them in a social context. People love to be entertained, wined and dined, just as much as you or I, and every client wants to think of his lawyer as "just a regular person, not that much different than me once he gets out of the office."

Be assured: when you are taken to lunch, cocktails or dinner you are being subjected to the most intense scrutiny, as here more than anywhere else you will demonstrate whether or not you are a good fit for that particular firm, corporation or government agency. I always find these interviews to be the most stressful, in fact, because I cannot rely on my technical skills and hard working nature to pull me through; in this environment I live or die on my social skills and my ability to deal with people. So DON'T RELAX; you are under a microscope during this interview, and you will have to pull off the performance of your life if you want to get a job offer from these people who are wining and dining you.

C.   *Developing Social Skills*

To survive in a legal job interview, you must develop (if you do not already have them), certain social skills that your years in school and nonlegal jobs have never given you the opportunity to develop. If you are like most people (including me), your education has overlooked a number of social niceties that our forefathers (and sophisticated businesspeople and lawyers who inhabit the society you are about to enter) took for granted.

You have drunk much wine in your time, but you do not know a Bordeaux from a Haut Medoc. You really do not understand what all of the forks next to your plate are for. You are not conversant in many of the topics that frequently come up at business luncheons. You do not know how to dance the basic ballroom steps. You do not know the courses in a formal dinner (quick, which comes first, the meat or the fish course?).

This may sound like "finishing school" stuff to you at first; you may ask yourself "are all clients as sophisticated as all that? Won't they appreciate someone who is just one of the guys (or gals)?" Perhaps, but you cannot take that chance. In my experience, most business clients are pretty sophisticated, and a lawyer always wants to be sure he can "hold his own" socially with just about anyone, even if that someone is listed on the Social Register and has the bluest blood on Earth.

Rest assured that if your client is not very sophisticated, he will do everything in his power (if he has the money) to appear sophisticated in business circles. This is why so many "nouveau riche" businesspeople, like many of the takeover artists of the 1980s, took pains to marry wealthy, Social Register type spouses, joined the boards of local charities (especially in the arts and cultural fields), and furnished their townhouses or summer homes with works by prominent artists.

D.   The Importance of Correct Behavior

When you enter the lawyer's world, you will usually find yourself taking a step (or more than a step) up the social ladder as well. One of the first lessons you must learn is that social conversation among business colleagues or clients is never relaxed and informal; you cannot let your hair down and "be yourself." This is not a fraternity house mixer or a brew after work with your old college chums. There is a certain expectation of how you will behave, what you will say, what you will do, and how much you will drink (if you drink at all). You must learn and master the skills necessary to survive in your new setting. In the luncheon interview, as in any other legal job interview setting, you must send the interviewers a signal that you are one of them, that you belong. This chapter will give you a few suggestions that will help you get ahead of the competition.

1.   *What Do You Talk About?*

First, you must be able to carry on a conversation. And not about just anything. For some reason, there are a number of topics that seem to come up again and again during business lunches and other professional social engagements: the current state of the economy (or of a particular industry), the current state of the legal profession, sports, automobiles, real estate, the performing arts, vacations, and food (including wine).

Subjects that never seem to come up during business lunches (and should be avoided like the plague) include: your personal life (especially your romantic activities), shopping, clothes, hobbies that are unrelated to your profession, and scholarly topics. If it is possible to generalize, the topics that come up during business social occasions fall into one of two categories: (1) topics that demonstrate that the speakers take a broader view of their work than would be apparent if they interacted only at the office; and (2) "safe" topics that demonstrate that the speakers are just normal, everyday folks with the same basic interests as everyone else. If you have never owned a house or a condo in your life, and couldn't care less about sports or automobiles, you have much learning to do.

No matter how intensely you work, you simply must find the time to learn what is going on in the world. You must subscribe to a good daily newspaper -- one with strong sections on world events, business and the economy, sports, and cultural affairs. When in doubt, there are two standbys: The New York Times and The Wall Street Journal. I would recommend that you have the paper delivered to your home, so that you can read it over breakfast or on your way to work; you don't want to clutter up the business day with reading.

I would also recommend that you subscribe to one of the "better" magazines that offer insights and analysis on the stories you are reading about in your daily newspaper. I personally find Atlantic, Harper's (not, and I emphatically mean NOT, Harper's Bazaar) and The New Yorker to be the best of these; Time, Newsweek and U.S. News and World Report, while they served you well in college and law school, will not be as useful as they simply rehash the stories from the previous week's daily newspaper -- you cannot afford to be more than a day or two out of touch.

If your education on houses, automobiles, cultural matters or sports is weak, I would recommend subscribing to a publication that treats these subjects in a nontechnical way: Sports Illustrated, for example, or Car and Driver. Finally, if you know you are having lunch with someone who has a peculiar passion or interest, try to read up on it as much as you can before the luncheon interview so that you can put him at ease and get him to hold forth on something he dearly loves (who knows? you may even learn something yourself).

This may seem trite to you, but I have found that being able to converse on a variety of topics (especially if they are the "right" ones for your environment) enhances your self-confidence. Remember that you are not trying to become an expert; your goal, as during a more formal job interview, is to be able to ask intelligent questions, demonstrate to other people that you share their interests, and "open up" the interviewers so that they do as much of the talking as possible.

2.   *Know Your Way Around The Menu*

A luncheon interview, of course, is more than just talk. There is eating and drinking going on as well, and you must have some knowledge of food, wine and spirits. Most of the fancy restaurants to which you will be taken for luncheon or dinner interviews will feature French or Italian (particularly northern Italian) cuisine: it will help for you to study a couple of cookbooks so that you can understand the menu.

When I first started interviewing, I befriended the maitre d' of one of New York's better French restaurants, who for a few dollars on the side walked me through most of the menu items that are staples at French restaurants -- told me which ones the "tourists" ate, which ones require special utensils (escargot, or snails, usually have to be removed from their shells, and it takes practice to master the special removing tool that the waiter will silently place in front of you with a knowing smile), and which ones should be avoided at all costs (even a seasoned interviewer will gag if the waiter brings a boiled sheep's brain to your seat, no matter how much you may protest your love of this delicacy).

3.   *Rules Regarding Liquor*

As for wine and spirits generally, different rules prevail depending on whether the interview is a luncheon, a cocktail session or a dinner. For a luncheon interview, the rule is simply stated: DON'T DRINK ANYTHING . . . PERIOD. When the waiter asks if you want "something to drink", ask for a club soda with lime or a plain tonic water, and don't worry about what the other folks are drinking. No one will question your choice; these days a lot of people are avoiding alcohol altogether, and if anyone does ask you can always say "I have a long afternoon ahead of me, and I want to keep a clear head."

If your interview is taking place over cocktails, the general rule is: THE LESS EXOTIC, THE BETTER. This is not a place for Pina Coladas or any fancy concoction that comes with a little umbrella. Because it is a cocktail, you must drink something; if you are uncomfortable drinking alcoholic beverages, you can always order a light beer or a club soda with lime. If you must drink something alcoholic, my recommendation is Scotch and water, or Scotch and soda (if you want to impress your interviewer, you can ask that it be made with an upscale brand of Scotch, such as Chivas Regal or Dewar's White Label -- they all taste the same). My experience is that it takes many Scotches before you start to feel any adverse effects, and even if you do you are unlikely to have a serious hangover the next morning.

If you cannot stand the taste of Scotch (many people can't -- it tastes vaguely like iodine, and is definitely an acquired taste), order a Bourbon and water, a Bourbon and soda, or a Bourbon and ginger ale instead (Bourbon has a sweeter taste, more like brandy); if you want to impress your interviewer here, you can order a Bourbon by name (popular brands are Jack Daniel's and Jim Beam -- avoid asking for Wild Turkey, as it tends to be associated with Rednecks and honky tonks) or by state (Bourbon is often known as Kentucky or Tennessee whisky). You should avoid martinis and Manhattans -- even if your interviewer is having one -- as these are strong drinks that can "knock you for a loop" even if you limit yourself to one.

A glass of wine or beer is an acceptable cocktail, but is not preferred, especially if you are having dinner with the interviewers immediately afterwards -- wine, especially, is something you drink with dinner, and an interviewer may think you are unimaginative or unsophisticated if you stay with wine the entire evening.

Finally, to repeat a point, unless you are interviewing in Honolulu, do not order a Hawaiian drink. If the bar is one that is famous for these, you can always return to the bar after your interviewing is done and indulge to your heart's content.

4.   *The Wine List*

For a dinner interview, the order of the day (or evening) is wine. I have learned that it helps to know something about wine in the business world, but you need not become an expert. A useful beginner's guide to the world of fine wines is Kevin Zraly's *Complete Windows on the World Wine Course*, which you will find in paperback at just about any bookstore for under $15. Once you have tasted some of the more common red and white wine labels in Zraly's book, you will usually be able to order from a wine list with confidence.

Remember: (1) red wines with meat, white wines with fish or chicken, and (2) the lighter the meat's color, the lighter the red wine's taste should be (for beef a hearty Burgundy or Cabernet Sauvignon is best, for lamb or veal a lighter Merlot, Rose or even a Zinfandel is better). Sweet wines are to be avoided, unless there is a need to comply with special dietary needs.

After a dinner interview, the drink of choice is Brandy or Cognac; most people order these by name brand, so it may help if you familiarize yourself beforehand with one or two of the most common brands (such as Courvoisier, Martell or Remy Martin).

5.   *What Do You Order?*

Now let's turn to food. I will assume that you have done your homework and can identify the dishes on the menu (nothing, I mean nothing, is more embarrassing than ordering something off the menu with a fancy name, only to discover when it arrives on your plate that it looks absolutely disgusting).

What should you order from the menu? Should you order the most expensive dish on the menu or one of the less expensive "specials"? Should you order first or after your interviewers have ordered? Should you order what they order? These are questions that will inevitably cross your mind when the waiter comes around to take orders, and there are no easy answers. Let's take them one at a time.

Should you order the most expensive dish on the menu or one of the less expensive "specials"? This is a tough one. During the heyday of the 1980s on Wall Street I would have said "order one of the restaurant's specialties, even if it is one of the most expensive things on the menu; this will tell the interviewers you are sophisticated and courageous, not easily intimidated, with a hearty appetite for life." In these more frugal times, where clients audit every penny of their legal bills, my advice would be "don't order the cheapest thing on the menu, but be a little sensitive to price, as the interviewers will not want to hire someone who runs up a client's bill need-

lessly." In any case, you should order something you like and
are comfortable eating; otherwise you will spend too much time
trying to figure out how to eat your entree when you should be
focusing on the conversation.

Should you order first or after your interviewers have
ordered? I prefer to order after my interviewers have ordered,
as this will give me a chance to determine if they are inclined to
pinch pennies or "go for the gusto", and I then follow their lead
with a greater likelihood of success. The trick, of course, is to
do this without being too obvious about it. A technique I have
used successfully is to not even look at my menu until the
waiter aproaches the table to take orders, making believe I am
totally absorbed in the conversation. When the interviewers
ask me if I'd like to order, I say "you know, I've been so
involved I haven't had a chance to even look at the menu.
Why don't you go ahead; I'll be ready by the time you're
finished ordering?" Then, by listening to what is being ordered, I will know how best to fit in with the group.

Should you order what they order? In a word, "never".
You never order anything one of your interviewers is eating,
especially if you are ordering after they have ordered. Doing
so demonstrates a lack of imagination, or too great a willingness
to "follow the crowd". In scanning the menu, you should have
a first, second and third choice, and go with your highest
priority that has not been ordered by one of the other persons at
the table. If you simply must order something that one of the
interviewers is eating, because it is a personal favorite or a
world-renowned specialty of that restaurant, try to differentiate
your order by asking for a different side dish, or (if it is a meat
dish) asking to have it cooked differently, and then be sure to
tell the interviewers that "I couldn't come to this restaurant and
not have the [whatever]!"

6.   *Table Manners and Etiquette*

This is not the place to discuss table manners and etiquette; suffice it to say that you should know what you are doing. If you are being interviewed at a formal dinner (this is unlikely), you will need to know the traditional courses, and the traditional order in which they are served. You will need to know which fork to use, and how to place your utensils on your plate when you are done. There are books that teach such things, and you must not only read them but practice until you don't even have to think about doing the right thing.

7.   *If You Are Left Handed*

If you are left handed, be sure the waiter or maitre d' knows this when you are being seated; at a good restaurant the waiter will know (or will be told) to furnish you with a left handed table setting. Also, if the table is such that two or more people must sit on the same side, be sure to sit yourself in such a way that there is no interviewer seated to your immediate left. If you fail to do this (and the interviewer to your immediate left is right handed), your left arm will be constantly poking that interviewer in the ribs.

CHAPTER 6

NEGOTIATING THE "TANGIBLES"

A.   *What Are "Tangibles"?*

Up to now, we have been talking about legal job interviews that take place before an offer of employment is made. The emphasis has been on convincing your prospective employer that you are the best available "fit" for the job. Once an offer has been made, there will inevitably be some discussion of "tangibles" such as salary, pension and health care benefits, perquisites, and the size and location of your office. Rarely if ever will these items be discussed in detail prior to a job offer being extended (and you should never, ever, ever bring them up before you have an offer firmly in hand; it is an instant turn-off to an interviewer, signaling as it does that you are a money-power-and-status grubber who really does not care about the work or the employer's needs).

Once an offer is on the table, however, it is expected that there will be some discussion of the "tangibles" that will go with the position, and some give-and-take is not only expected, but is budgeted for. How much negotiation is sufficient? The answer will of course depend on the job, your employer's willingness to be flexible, and your needs for certain "tangibles". There are, however, two "rules of thumb" which can be stated categorically: (1) the candidate for a job who accepts an offer immediately without any discussion of "tangibles" is demonstrating his insecurity, his lack of self-esteem, and therefore his unsuitability for the position; and (2) the candidate who negotiates too hard and too long over "tangibles" (especially the less important ones) is demonstrating his unwillingness to follow orders, his inability to become a "team player", and therefore his unsuitability for the position.

This is going to be a short chapter, for two reasons. First, this is one of the few areas in which the general, nonlegal books on interviewing skills excel, and you will be well served by looking up one or more of these books for guidance in specific situations. Second, and more important for the legal job interviewee, is that for most legal positions (1) there aren't a whole lot of "tangibles" available (other than a higher-than-average salary and some prestige) and (2) the employer's room for negotiation is usually quite limited. In a law firm, for example, salary increments are usually based on the number of years a lawyer has spent working since he graduated from law school (and sometimes not even then: at one large law firm in New York City there are currently four classes of associates who all make the same salary).

It would be very bad form for a law firm to pay a fifth-year associate (even an outstanding one) more than it pays its sixth-year associates. Moreover, the difference or "spread" between the fifth and sixth year salaries is likely to be only a couple of thousand dollars, which limits severely the firm's ability to negotiate a special deal for a highly desirable candidate. While this is beginning to change at some of America's largest law firms, the traditional "lock step" salary curve is likely to remain for quite some time.

What this chapter will do is summarize some of the most important lessons I have learned in negotiating "tangibles" once a firm job offer has been made.

B.   *Rule 1: "I Want", Not "Can I Have?"*

When asking for a better "tangibles" package than the one offered by a prospective employer, the preferred approach is to be polite but assertive. Being too bashful, or too mindful of the interviewer's emotional needs, at this point in the game will set you back in a big way. The interviewer, who up to now has been totally charmed out of his socks by your presentation, now begins to think you lack the self-confidence necessary to become a successful lawyer (sad but true: a lawyer who is afraid of polite confrontation is not destined to be among the great ones) and may be tempted to re-open the interview to make sure his judgment about you is really correct.

While asking for something more than is "on the table" must be done in a way that is consistent with your own style, I believe it is better to do it in the form of declarative sentences describing what you want in the way of "tangibles" than to ask for a better "tangibles" package in the form of a question. For example, let's say a prospective employer has made you an offer at a salary slightly below your expectations. If you respond to the news by saying "your offer is most generous, Joe, but do you think it is possible you could go up a few thousand?", here are some of the things your prospective employer may be thinking: "he hasn't really rejected my initial offer; if I say 'no' to this request he'll probably still take it"; "what makes him think he's worth an extra few thousand?; he's just as good as any of our other fifth-year associates, and they don't make anything more than my initial offer"; "he's made it too easy for me to say 'no'; do I really want someone like this negotiating multimillion dollar deals for my streetwise clients?"

A better approach might be to say something like "I think your offer of $70,000 per year is a good one, Joe, but I was hoping for something more in the range of $80,000 in light of my special expertise in this area and my recent stint with the government agency which regulates most of your clients." Here your prospective employer has a tougher time saying "no": you have given him a reason to pay you more than other employees who are similarly situated; you haven't really rejected the initial offer but you have sent a strong signal that your expectations were higher and that the employer should "reach" a little bit if he wants to get you; and you have sent an even stronger signal that this is an offer you can afford to walk away from (the importance of this will be discussed below under "Rule 2").

C.   Rule 2: *"You Can Only Get A Bargain On Something You Don't Really Want"*

This advice, incidentally, is from my Mother, one of the all-time great department store shoppers. What it means, simply, is that the more you really want or need something, the less you will risk losing the deal by negotiating aggressively and assertively. You should determine early on if this is a job you really want, a job you would not want under any circumstances, or one which attracts you in a lukewarm way (the job offer will fall in this last category if you find yourself saying "it's a good job, but there are some negatives so if I don't get it I won't lose any sleep"). Knowing how much (or how little) the proffered job means to you will largely determine your clout when negotiating the "tangibles" of the job.

If you have been out of work for a year or more, and someone offers you a job at half your previous salary but enough to pay the grocer and make your mortgage and car payments, you will be hard pressed to ask for more (even though you may well get more in this situation if you ask for it, as an interviewer is likely to be very impressed by your courage in such a desperate situation). Similarly, if you have been offered a job that nobody but a fool would refuse at a salary that would make anyone green with envy, it will be hard to ask your employer to "gild the lily" (chances are, however, that if you have been made such an offer it is because you are a very special or unique person who probably can get more if you ask for it because there's only one of you available). Unless you are very good at "bluffing" and concealing how much you want or need the position, you will likely end up working on the terms set by your prospective employer.

The converse is also true: the less you want a job, the easier it is to play hardball when negotiating the "tangibles" (after all, any job is worth doing at the right price). Early in my youth, in my last year of college, I interviewed for a sales position with a major radio network. The interviewer, who would have been my boss, dressed in a sharkskin suit, wore an obvious toupee and the loudest tie I had ever seen, talked like a gangster, used an obvious "stage" name in his business dealings, and had a faint musty odor about him.

Moreover, it soon became clear to me that success in the position would involve incredibly long hours in a very political environment where the prevailing motto was "sell the customer no matter what you have to tell him", and absolutely no personal contact with customers or other salespeople. Even worse, the opening needed to be filled immediately, so I would have been forced to leave college early, before getting my diploma, to take the job. I decided early on that I was not interested in the position, and pushed the interviewer to bring the interview to an end early so that neither of us would waste the other's time.

Well, little did I know that that is the worst tactic to use with an aggressive salesperson; the more I resisted, the more he wanted me for the job. Before I knew it, I had an offer, which I promptly rejected. He then doubled the salary, on the spot. I again said no. The salary went up again. This time I excused myself and left the office; he followed me down the hall and into the street, sweetening the offer. The son-of-a-gun kept calling me at home, late at night, for three weeks afterward, and each time the salary kept going up until the original offer had quintupled. By this time, I admit, he was getting close to a number to which I couldn't say no. But he didn't quite get there, and I didn't budge, so eventually he gave up. The moral of the story is that I did not then, and have never since, lost a moment of sleep worrying about what might have happened had I taken the job. It was easy for me to walk away from the situation (contrary to what the salesperson thought, I honestly did not want the job), and so it was easy for me to negotiate.

D.   *Rule 3: Noncash "Tangibles" Are Easier To Negotiate Than Cash "Tangibles"*

The first item on anyone's list of "tangibles" is, of course, salary. Salary is a "tangible" that requires an employer to fork over cash to you on a regular basis. Cash is scarce, even in good times. What do you do when you and your employer are close to agreement on salary, but it appears that the employer has gone as high as he can go?

There are some very valid reasons why an employer can go only so high on salary and no further. He may only be authorized to go up to a certain figure for the position. If he is to be your future boss, he does not want you making more than he does himself. If there are others working at the same level for the employer, he does not want your salary to be grossly out of line with theirs (somehow the word always gets out, and it's bad for morale).

When this point has been reached, there are three possible solutions: (1) you cave in (and possibly lose face with the employer); (2) you indicate that you will accept the offer only at the higher salary (thereby forcing your interviewer to lose you or "put himself on the line" by making an extraordinary effort in his organization to win approval for the higher salary for you -- can you guess which way most interviewers will go?); or (3) you suggest a "tradeoff" that will get you something you want and save your interviewer's face. If you desperately need the job, you take alternative (1); if you really don't care whether you get the job or not, you take alternative (2); and if you are disposed to take the job but not entirely on the employer's terms, you adopt alternative (3). How do you go about executing option (3)?

One way is to suggest that while the lower amount can be your "base salary", it can and should be supplemented by some sort of incentive compensation based on your performance; that way, your employer is required to pay you the higher amount only if through your efforts there is more money to go around for everybody. This is a common approach for businesspeople whose performance and results can easily be quantified (such as salespeople). It is a much more difficult approach for lawyers, whose contribution to an employer is often less tangible (how can you quantify the amount an employer has saved in litigation costs or regulatory penalties because your expert lawyering has prevented it from making a serious and costly mistake?). Still, in most law firms these days you should be able to negotiate a percentage -- over and above base salary -- of the firm's receivables from clients which you introduce to the firm.

A better approach for legal professionals is to suggest a noncash "tangible" -- one that does not require an immediate or regular outlay of cash -- in lieu of the higher salary. A window office, for example, versus an interior office (or a private office as opposed to a shared office). An earlier performance review than would otherwise be the case (the implication here being that the "gap" between your salary position and that of your employer can be bridged several months hence, when the employer will have a better sense of your value). Perhaps an extra few days of vacation time, or an assurance that you will do a particularly exciting and visible type of work. The key is to want the job enough to be willing to live with the (hopefully temporarily) lower salary.

Generally, this approach is easier when you are interviewing for a corporate job -- they have a wider variety of benefits and perquisites and thus there is more you can get in such a "tradeoff" -- than when you are interviewing for a job with a law firm or a government agency. Law firms are not known for offering a wide variety of benefits (most of the larger ones view the high salary and prestige of working there as sufficient inducements -- a few regrettably don't want you to stick around and accordingly have no incentive to make your life at the firm comfortable -- and the smaller ones are usually so focused on the bottom line that they cannot afford a wide line of benefits), while government agencies are often required by civil service laws to offer the same "tangibles" -- without negotiation -- to all applicants for a position at a particular level to avoid discrimination and other undesirable social effects.

E.   Rule 4: Do Your Homework and Know What Is Gettable

Keep in mind that how aggressively you negotiate the "tangibles" will depend to some extent on the relative bargaining power of you and your prospective employer. If you are interviewing for your first legal job with a large and powerful law firm, you will most likely have to "take the standard package" without much negotiation (unless you are an editor of the Harvard Law Review, graduating first in your class, with a parent who is the chief executive office of the firm's most important client). If you have developed a specialty in a "hot" area of practice and have portable clients who will guarantee $1,000,000 or more in annual billings, and you are interviewing to become partner of a small firm that needs to grow, the balance of negotiating power is quite different; your interviewer may be willing to give you his own office if it means bringing you on board!

Before the "tangibles" stage of the interview is reached, it is best if you do your homework. Talk to others who occupy similar positions at similar organizations in the same geographic area, and find out what is customary and what is not. This will help you gauge more accurately whether the initial offer is "within the ballpark" or a "lowball" that can be improved. Make sure your requests are realistic and have at least some precedent for the type of organization with which you are interviewing. Do not ask for a company car when interviewing for a law firm; nobody has a company car at a law firm (this can, however, be a negotiable item when interviewing for a corporate legal job).

F.   *Rule 5: Remember That You Are Still Interviewing*

Finally, when asking for more than the interviewer is initially willing to give, be sure you give your interviewer good reasons for wanting more (this will help your interviewer justify his concession to himself, his superiors and his colleagues). Remember that your interviewer is your "partner" in helping you get what you want, and he will not do this unless he (and his organization) is simultaneously getting what he wants. Keep stressing your unique achievements that make you a better "fit" for the position than anyone else, your better potential to market the firm to prospective clients, your wealth of connections, your mastery of environmental law, whatever it takes.

CHAPTER 7

STRATEGIES FOR ANSWERING SOME COMMONLY ASKED INTERVIEWING QUESTIONS

During the course of a legal job interview, you can expect to be asked numerous questions about your background, your experience, and your personal interests, as the interviewer attempts to determine in his own mind whether or not you would be a good "fit" for his organization. Keep in mind that whenever a question is asked, the interviewer really intends to ask another -- more difficult, more personal -- question that the interviewing rules of etiquette (or his own conscience) prevent him from asking you directly. When framing your answer to an interviewer's question, you must first determine the question you are really being asked, and then answer the question in a way that both (A) responds to the "surface" question and (B) furnishes the information the interviewer is really after.

Let's look at some typical interview questions and see how you might be able to structure your answers. Note that I do not believe in "form answers" for two reasons. First, everyone is different, and a "form answer" that works for many people may not be convincing in your case. Second, it will be only a matter of time before interviewers get around to reading this book, and they will be suspicious if your answer sticks too closely to the suggested format. Sadly, there are no easy ways or shortcuts to answering interview questions; you must develop your own, write them down, and make sure you can deliver the words in a sincere, convincing way.

Accordingly, this chapter will not furnish you with "form answers", but rather provide an analysis of the interview question and a structure or outline of the "right" answer that you can then flesh out in your own way. In each case I will try to identify what I think is the "hidden" question underlying the "surface" question, and illustrate how I think you can answer both questions with a single answer.

Why Did You Decide To Become A Lawyer? You can expect this question when interviewing for your first job out of law school, although it may crop up as well when you are looking to make a lateral move or a career change. The question the interviewer really wants to ask here is "did you make this decision consciously, with knowledge of what the legal profession is all about, or did you just follow the crowd or let other people make your career decision for you?" In other words, the interviewer wants to know if you are self-directed or other-directed.

No matter what the truth of the situation, you want to provide an answer that shows you are self-directed, that you did your homework before applying to law school, you know what you have gotten yourself into, and you can live with the legal profession's shortcomings. Do not under any circumstances say, "my father (or mother) is a lawyer" or "I didn't know what else to do with myself, and the law opens up so many different career paths" or "I was attracted by the money and the power," even if these are truthful answers in your case. Similarly, your answer should not be framed as a variation on the theme "I wanted to help other people," as there are many other professions in which that can be done.

Your answer should send the interviewer a strong signal that you wanted to become a lawyer: that you were attracted by the intellectual stimulation which a legal career affords; that you knew a lot of lawyers growing up and were fascinated by their stories of what they did day-to-day; that you did a report in grade school on a famous legal case that turned you on for life. Your answer should not sound contrived or "hokey", but it will go over well if you can give your answer a personal twist.

An answer I have occasionally used when this question is asked goes something like this: "well, Mr. So-and-So, when I was in college I knew I wanted a profession that would give me intellectual stimulation, but I couldn't see myself as a college professor; that was too abstract for me. What I love about the law is that it is a very cerebral and scholarly profession, and yet my actions and decisions are having an impact in the real world. I took a couple of Legal Studies courses in college, and that cemented my decision that this is what I wanted to do with my life."

What Sorts Of Courses Have You Enjoyed The Most In Law School? Again, you can expect this question more when you are interviewing for your first legal job. The question the interviewer really wants to ask is "what area(s) of practice are you interested in, and will we be able to accommodate your preference(s)?" You should not answer that you enjoyed courses in an area that is alien to the employer's practice. For example, if your passion is bankruptcy work, you should not bring this up when you are interviewing with a firm that does no bankruptcy work (although you should ask yourself why you are interviewing with such a firm in the first place? Methinks you have not done the homework Chapter 3 told you you must do before a legal job interview).

Your research and homework before the interview will give you some idea of the firm's strongest practices, and which ones have the strongest potential for long-term growth. These areas should form the backbone of your answer. If in fact you have not taken any courses in these areas (because, let's say, they are third year courses and you are interviewing for a second year summer clerkship), you should say so, thusly: "well, the course I'm looking most forward to is antitrust, but I held off taking it until the third year because the prerequisites for that course are all second year courses and I wanted to get these done first."

In your legal career you will have to make a decision fairly early on about whether you will become a litigator (either at the trial or appellate level) handling cases, or a legal counselor (such as a corporate lawyer or a "trusts and estates" specialist) whose practice consists mostly of office work. If you are not careful this decision will be made for you when you are assigned to your first department within the firm. If you are not sure which approach will give you long term career satisfaction, your answer should signal your desire to experience both types of practice at the earliest possible time, so that you can make an informed decision as early as possible.

Why Are You Looking To Join a [Big Firm] [Small Firm] [Corporation] At This Point In Your Career? This question can be asked in almost any interview setting. Your answer must be carefully crafted, because the question the interviewer wants to ask is "do you know enough about the different legal environments that I can count on your having a long-term commitment to my employer?" Interviewers have a general distaste for job hoppers, but they really dislike people who demonstrate that they have not "found themselves" professionally. Your answer must show some research, and should persuade the interviewer that your career horizons are long term.

What is more, if you are changing jobs, you must be able to demonstrate why a different environment would be a better "fit" than your present one. Your answer to this question must fit perfectly with your answer to the question "why do you want to make a change at this point?", which is discussed below.

Your answer to this question will depend on the type of move you are trying to make. If you are looking to switch from a law firm environment to a corporation, for example, you will have to stress a desire to get closer to the business side of things (there are many who think that in-house corporation lawyers do not really practice law at all but are pseudo-businesspeople) and represent one client instead of many.

If you are looking to switch from a corporation to a law firm, your emphasis will be just the opposite: you want to be "more of a lawyer," develop expertise in a particular area of practice, and represent a variety of clients instead of just one.

If your move is from a large law firm to a smaller one, you want to stress the desire to work on a variety of matters instead of just a few specialized transactions, and to work on an entire (albeit much smaller) matter from beginning to end rather than working on a very small piece of a very large matter. Your expression of a desire to "get closer to the clients, and be more of a full-service counselor to them" may also be helpful.

If you are looking to move from a small large firm to a larger one, you will emphasize your desire to work on a higher quality of matter, become an expert in your field, experience a greater intellectual challenge, and deal with more sophisticated clients. If you can say it honestly, and if the firm has the reputation for being one of the best in your chosen field, you can say something like "frankly, I won't consider myself a successful bankruptcy lawyer until I am working at your firm, because you are the best in the business, and I want to be known as one of the best bankruptcy lawyers around."

If you are interviewing for your first legal job, you can avail yourself of any of the above strategies for answering this question. Interviewers will be most interested in your commitment to a particular geographic area (discussed below), will be somewhat less concerned about your desired area of practice (most large firms will allow you to rotate among several departments in your first few years in practice, and most smaller firms and corporations have a more generalized practice anyway where specialization will be discouraged), and will think it premature for you to be worried about being an "expert" versus being "closer to the business side of things."

Why Do You Want To Make A Change At This Point In Your Career? This question is certain to be asked in a lateral hiring or career changing situation; the interviewer looking at entry level job candidates will fully understand why you want to get out of law school and start making some money! Note that this question is the flip side of "what are you looking for in a [small firm] [large firm] [corporation]?" In that case you are being asked to identify the things that interest you in a different environment. In this case you are being asked to identify what you think is wrong about your current environment.

You have to handle this one very carefully; this is a question that should never be answered too honestly or candidly. It's a funny thing about human nature, but when you knock your current employer you end up knocking yourself much worse in the interviewer's eyes. Nobody (and I mean nobody) likes a whiner or a complainer; every job has its bad days and its negative aspects, and the position for which you are applying is no different.

One of the worst things you can do in a legal job interview is to cite as a negative aspect of your current situation something that the interviewer thinks pertains equally well to the position you are applying for! Your reason for leaving your current employer must be stated in positive terms: it is not so much that your "fit" with your current employer is not so good, but rather that you see the opportunity for a much better "fit" with the interviewer's employer. How to convince an interviewer that this in fact so? In particular, how do you do this when in fact you have been fired from your previous employer and are currently unemployed?

First, you should never admit that you are "between jobs." Before leaving the employer that fired you, you should get your former boss to agree that when discussing you with your prospective new employer, the former boss will use a "termination story" showing either that you left of your own accord (even though this is not strictly speaking true) or that you were let go because of circumstances beyond the control of either you or your former boss. Usually, this "termination story" will say either that you left of your own free will to pursue new opportunities with the old employer's blessing, because of your mutual perception of a less than perfect "fit" with that employer, or that your position was slated for elimination at some point in time (that has not been reached yet -- always keep moving it out into the future so that it appears you are still employed) and you expressed a desire to "take a look around and see what the market is like right now."

Most bosses will agree to this. Why, you may ask? Because it helps them avoid lawsuits from terminated employees if they "play ball" to a certain extent. Besides, in a termination situation it is always best for both sides not to burn their bridges behind them. The legal profession is an incestuous one, and no matter how hard you try to avoid brushing up against people you knew professionally in the past, you will be constantly bumping into them -- when working on transactions, when sitting on bar association committees, at social functions, and so forth. Who knows? In your next job you may become the world's leading expert in a narrow area of specialization that takes off and becomes the hottest thing since leveraged buyouts in the 1980s. Your old firm may have to refer business to you! In law as in life, excellence is always the best revenge.

Once you have gotten your former boss to agree on the "termination story", you are in a much better position to answer the question "why are you changing jobs right now?". You simply repeat the story that you and your former boss have agreed on.

Let's say you have not been terminated but are simply "looking around" for a better opportunity. If you are looking at a different legal environment, your answer will track exactly your answer to the question "why are you looking for a [small firm] [large firm] [corporation]?," which is discussed above. Nothing more, nothing less. If you are looking to move to a similar environment in a different geographic location, your answer will track exactly your answer to the question "why do you want to come to [name of city or town]?", which is discussed below. Nothing more, nothing less. In either case, your answer is framed in terms of what YOU want to do, because of a decision YOU have made.

What if you are looking to move to a similar environment in the same geographic location? In other words, what if you are considering a move to a competing firm or corporation (I take the view, which some may dispute, that all law firms of a similar size in the same city are competitors)? Your answer to this question will have to include a paean to the superior practice or opportunity for professional development that is available at the new employer, which does not simultaneously knock down your current employer. You may want to say something like "after working on a variety of matters at Firm P, I have come to the conclusion that I want to make bankruptcy practice my life's work; while Firm P has a pretty good bankruptcy practice, as everyone knows, I think the opportunities for bankruptcy lawyers at your firm is much greater, because you are recognized as practicing bankruptcy law at a much higher level than just about anyone in this city."

In all of these situations, you must accentuate the positive, and eliminate the negative. What you have is good (or at least you are not unhappy with what you have); what you want is better.

Note that in none of these situations do you give the desire for a "lifestyle change" as an answer to the question "why do you want to change jobs?" You never, ever, ever want to appear burned out in front of a legal job interviewer. Lawyering is hard work, no matter where you practice, no matter what type of law you practice, no matter what your legal environment. The hours are long, and unpredictable.

By stressing the need for a "lifestyle change" you are in effect answering the question as follows: "I have tried my best to keep up with the demanding pace in my current position, but

I just can't do it. I want to slow down, take things easier, have more time for myself, and develop at my own pace." While this may be a totally sincere answer, the interviewer cannot help but think that what you really want is an "early retirement" or a part-time law practice that will provide the financial security necessary for you to do other things that you find more interesting and challenging. Neither interpretation of your answer will help your cause. You must always appear to the interviewer to be a bright, hard working, go getter, even if you and he would agree (in a perfect world) that the pace of work at his firm is indeed much slower than it is at your current employer.

The one possible exception (note I say "possible") to the rule that "lifestyle change" is never to be given as an answer to this question is where you are a new parent who feels he must adjust his work schedule to perform his child care duties. There is a growing awareness of the need for "flextime" in such situations, and some employers (not nearly all, nor even a majority) have begun to create "mommy tracks" that enable new parents (almost exclusively mothers -- there is a certain amount of sexism in the application of "mommy tracks", and for the time being I would advise against a male requesting such a thing) to reduce their workload during their children's early years while still being taken seriously as a candidate for advancement and professional development.

I would argue, however, that even in such a situation, where your current employer is not as sensitive to this issue as your prospective new employer would be, you should stress your commitment to the profession and your desire to practice in a different environment that will be a better "fit" for you. Your status as a new parent can be communicated in other ways, and the message will be received without your having to make it obvious.

Why Do You Want To Come To [Name Of City Or Town]? If you are looking to move to a different geographic area, you will have to explain your reason for moving. You do not want to say that you are following a "trailing spouse," even if this is the case (what if the spouse gets transferred again in a couple of years? Remember that lawyers are looking for long term commitment). Nor do you want to say that you want to be closer to a girlfriend or boyfriend (there is no guarantee, after all, that your relationship will be stronger once you are closer together, and besides, giving this as a reason sends a signal to the prospective employer that you value your personal life over your career).

The best reasons for a geographic change, assuming they have some basis in reality, are (1) a desire to return to the area where you grew up or went to college, after having practiced in a distant location for several years, and (2) a desire to practice in a location that is world famous for a particular legal specialty that you want to make your own (a specialist in insurance law, for example, would be silly not to consider a stint in New York City or Hartford, Connecticut, where most of the large American insurance companies are based).

In the former case, you are signaling to the interviewer that your "roots" are strong, and that you are unlikely to move from the area once you have settled back in. In the latter case, you are demonstrating a strong commitment to a specialty that is unlikely to move away from that area for a very long time; by moving away from that area you would be sacrificing much in the quality of your practice.

What Will Your Current Boss Say When We Ask For A Reference? Until you started interviewing, you probably never realized that you would be asked to read someone else's mind. Usually when an employer offers you a job, it is conditioned upon a satisfactory reference from your current boss. Because of the fear of litigation, most employers are trained never to say bad things about an employee during a reference check. But you can never be sure your boss will know precisely the story you have told your prospective new employer. This is why it is best, in a termination situation, for you and your employer to sit down and review your "termination story" together as early as possible in the process, so that you both can get it straight later on (sometimes it is wise to commit the "story" to writing, and make sure you fax a copy to your current or former boss well in advance of a reference check so that he can be prepared).

Even where you have not been terminated but have simply accepted a position elsewhere, before you allow your new employer to call your current one you should sit down with your current boss, announce your intentions (only after you have gotten an offer, of course) and make sure you both get the "story" straight.

The interviewer who asks this question is looking for you to say something negative about your current boss (which would be a truly stupid thing to do), or to give an assessment of yourself that will prove to be different than what he hears when he calls your current boss for a reference. One way to defuse this question in a harmless way (at least, in a situation where you have not yet had a chance to prepare your current boss for the reference check) is to say something like "well, I hope he would say that I was a diligent, hard working, thorough and intelligent lawyer, because that's what he has always told me to date." That way, if your boss is foolish enough to say something less enthusiastic about you, it is your word against your boss' word. The interviewer still may choose to take your boss' word over yours, but at least you have not lied outright.

A word about reference checks. Many interview books place a lot of emphasis on these, and would lead you to believe that a prospective employer would turn you down, even after making you an offer, if your current boss' reference is anything less than an unqualified rave. In practice, however, it is very hard to tell if someone gives a less than enthusiastic reference because (1) he is genuinely unimpressed by the individual who has worked for him, or (2) he is genuinely upset that such a highly qualified individual is leaving him for employment elsewhere, and that he will have to begin the tedious process of replacing him. No interviewer will take the chance that his interpretation of the boss' reference is wrong, thereby saddling him with a possible lawsuit.

Accordingly, when answering this question it is always helpful if you can throw in a comment to the effect that "I suspect my current boss will be extremely upset to hear that I am leaving; we've always been so close, and he has been a terrific mentor to me." This will effectively defuse the question, as the interviewer will now have a strong reason to suspect the second interpretation of a less than enthusiastic reference. He will want to believe you, because doing otherwise will either (1) make him doubt his own judgment (a difficult thing for most people) or (2) compel him to back away from his previous commitment to you (which may cause him embarrassment within the organization).

Where Do You Want To Be Five (Or Ten) Years From Now? When an interviewer asks this question, he wants to know if you consider yourself to have the potential for reaching the top ranks of his organization (possibly knocking him out of contention along the way), and whether your career ambitions are realistic. An incorrect, although possibly sincere, answer to this question would be "I want to be a partner in your firm. Period." Five or ten years is a long time, after all, and people's goals and expectations change over that long a period of time; I think an interviewer would perceive such an answer as immature.

Another incorrect answer would be "Who knows? Five or ten years is a long time; I believe in going with the flow." Everybody has to have some goals in life, after all; I mean, if you don't plan on going anywhere, how do you know which way to go? How do you know that you really want to be a lawyer, if that is how you feel about things? I think an interviewer would perceive this answer as indicating a lack of goal setting ability, ambition and drive. Generally, Type B people (people who are relaxed, calm, and take each day as it comes) tend not to do well in legal environments, where Type A personalities (intense, driven, inclined to push themselves and those around them as hard as they can) tend to succeed in the long run.

In answering this question you should appear to be ambitious but realistic. A useful strategy for answering this question is to cast it in the form of "I want to be working in an environment that will make me happy", with the clarification that at least right now you think the interviewer's employer is such an environment. For example, you might want to say something like "I want to be practicing in an environment where I am constantly stimulated and challenged by the quality of the work (this, you can guess by now, is directed at the large firm), and where I can be a recognized expert in my chosen field of bankruptcy law; as your firm is recognized nationwide for the quality of its bankruptcy work, I would hope you would still want me around after all that time, and I think it's an environment that would make me very happy." Note that you have not said you want to be a partner; you have merely said that you want to be there still, doing the work you love. That's the kind of answer lawyer-interviewers like: one that demonstrates your long-term commitment to a line of work, but one that does not require a reciprocal commitment from the employer.

Keep in mind that your answer to this question must be tailored to the legal environment for which you are interviewing. The answer I have suggested above would not work with a smaller law firm, a government agency or a corporate legal department.

Do You Have Any Hobbies Or Outside Interests?
Beware! This question is a trap! In asking this question, the interviewer wants you to relax and tell him about all the things you love to do outside your work that you will no longer have any time to do once you start practicing law! I think this is probably the most dangerous "screening out" question an interviewer can ask, and you should approach it with kid gloves.

Above all, do not view this question as signaling the interviewer's sincere interest in your personal life. What he wants to hear is that you are just as much of a dull stick as he is, and therefore a perfect "fit" for his employer. The correct answer will signal two things to the interviewer: (1) that you really don't have many interests outside of your work; and (2) the few interests you have will help make you a better lawyer.

You might, for example, want to say something like "well, most of my time is tied up with work, and my family obligations take up most of the rest of my time. I do, however, love to read, and I play golf whenever I can." This tells the interviewer you will have few distractions from your work life, and the few distractions you will have are things of which he can approve. A good golf game will help you cement relationships with clients, and your work will involve more than a little bit of reading -- just don't admit to reading fiction, as a healthy imagination is not always considered a positive attribute in a good lawyer. If the interviewer asks you what you like to read, say "history" or "biography" or something else that shows your serious, logical, nonfrivolous side.

How Would You Describe Your Strengths? I have to believe that this question, and its companion "how would you describe your weaknesses?", are asked during ninety-nine percent of the legal job interviews conducted in the United States this year. You are virtually certain to be asked these two questions, so there is absolutely no excuse for you not to have an answer prepared in advance. One of the surest ways to screen yourself out in a legal job interview is to signal to your interviewer that these questions are coming as a surprise to you.

When the interviewer asks this question, he is looking to hear about things (1) that directly relate to the practice of law in his particular environment and (2) that he can use to sell you to his colleagues on the legal personnel committee, or to the other lawyers in the corporate legal department. An inappropriate answer would be "well, I once chugged fifteen consecutive cans of beer during a fraternity house party in college, so I guess you could say I hold my liquor well." While this may satisfy the interviewer's second criteria, it does not help him with the first.

A better answer can be structured something like this: "I love the intellectual challenge of the law, for the same reason I think I have always loved puzzles, games and mysteries of all kinds. I get so absorbed when I'm working on a problem that I totally lose track of time and cannot rest until I am comfortable I have the solution. I also have extremely strong people skills, and can get along with just about anybody. But most importantly, I know that [even though I have been doing this for a few years now] there is still a lot to learn, and probably always will be; I am not the sort of person ever to take my knowledge for granted." This tells the interviewer that you are detail oriented, are willing to do the work involved in finding a solution (note that I did not say "I cannot rest until I am comfortable I have found the answer"; finding the answer may be only the first step in solving a client's problem), and will not turn people (especially clients) off with your personality or bad habits. Finally, you have signaled your maturity (the law is always changing, and it is impossible to know everything there is about any area of practice) and humility in considering yourself a perpetual student of the law, one who does not "shoot from the hip" because he thinks he knows it all.

What Do You Consider To Be Your Most Serious Weaknesses? While this is probably the most dreaded question in any job interview, it is surprisingly easy to answer. When the interviewer asks this question, he hopes you will be naive enough actually to volunteer that you have weaknesses! This is probably the only interview question in which the "surface" question and the "real" question are one and the same, and the only one you can take at face value. Yet, it would not be the right answer to say, "well, I've given this a lot of thought, and I really can't think of any." Everybody has weaknesses; a failure to admit that is a sign of immaturity. How to answer this question without volunteering any weaknesses?

The key in answering this question is that what constitutes a "weakness" is simply a matter of perception. What you consider a personal weakness others may perceive as your strongest attribute. All you need to do when answering this question is to avoid mentioning anything that the interviewer perceives as a weakness, and use as the reason for screening you out. To put it differently, to answer this question correctly you must list one or two traits (never any more than that) that the interviewer is highly likely to regard as strengths, regardless of whether you actually view them as weaknesses.

You might, for example, want to say something like "well, a lot of people think I have an unbalanced life because I spend so much time on my work, and there are times I wish I could develop some more outside interests, but I take my work very seriously so that's awfully hard for me to do. As for other weaknesses, I guess you could say that I'm an impatient sort of person; I push myself very hard, and I sometimes get a little concerned when things aren't happening and there isn't much to do -- I have to be busy or else I'm not happy."

Tell me, what weaknesses have you demonstrated by this answer. Only that you are a hard charging workaholic with few outside interests and a desire to get things done. Guess what? As a successful lawyer, your interviewer shares these very weaknesses -- they are the very things (being intensely focused, having few distractions from the outside world, pushing himself hard to meet client deadlines and get the results the client wants) that have made him successful. There is no way he will view these attributes as weaknesses, so you have accomplished your task.

Of course, you must be able to say this sincerely and with feeling. Your acting ability counts for much here; if your interviewer thinks you are merely spewing out an answer you read in an interview book somewhere, it is all over for you. There are some interviewers, however, who actually look for this answer as a sign that you know what's going on in the world: I once had an interviewer tell me, "you know, Mr. Ennico, everybody gives that answer; and you know what? It's the only right answer to that question! Any other answer and you would blow yourself out of the water. You pass the 'stupid question' test; now let's get down to business."

Here's A Situation I'm Working On Right Now In the Office. What Would You Do If You Were In My Shoes? This is probably the most stressful question you can be asked during a legal job interview; the interviewer appears at first blush to seek proof of your technical competence. Actually, in most cases where the interviewer is not himself seeking free legal advice, he has a much different agenda. What is really wants to know is either (1) how you go about analyzing a difficult situation when it is first presented to you, much as a client would present it to you, or (2) how you handle a tough question when you know (and the interviewer knows) that you don't have the correct answer on the tip of your tongue. Will you bluff your way through and risk turning off the interviewer (or the client)? Will you take an "educated guess" and risk a malpractice lawsuit? Will you admit you don't know the answer and risk losing the client's confidence and trust? This question is full of potential landmines.

There is no one way to handle this type of question, but unless it is a situation you have encountered before and you know the answer right off (in which case you should not hesitate to demonstrate your expertise), the better approach is not to answer the question at all but show how you would go about finding the answer in a way that demonstrates you are thorough, cautious and not inclined to "shoot from the hip" under pressure.

I would begin by listening carefully to the facts given by the interviewer, and asking a couple of clarifying questions before putting together an answer. This shows your ability to focus on the important points -- the "operative facts" in the interviewer's hypothetical situation -- and screen out the irrelevant details, while also demonstrating to the interviewer that you do not rush to decisions.

If you are interviewing for your first job out of law school, and you really don't know anything about the area of law that applies to the interviewer's situation, your answer at this point is an easy one: "Mr. So-and-So, I can see that to answer this question thoroughly requires a knowledge of XXXX law, which is a course I have not yet taken, although I intend to [or "which we glossed over in my first year property course, and which I remember in a general way only"]. I would obviously not want to shoot from the hip, and would want to familiarize myself thoroughly with this area of the law, or seek help from other lawyers in the firm who specialize in that area, before attempting a definitive answer, certainly before giving the client advice on which he is going to rely."

If, however, you are applying for a lateral position or are seeking a career change, and if you have held yourself out as having some experience or expertise in the law relevant to the interviewer's question, you will have to take a stab at it. Once you have gotten all of the information you feel you need to attempt an analysis, I would begin by saying "of course, this is not the kind of question that has a 'hornbook' answer. To give a definitive answer, first, I would want to know more about [certain facts that have legal consequences].

Then, I would want to refresh myself on certain fine points of the law in this area, particularly [one or two statutes or leading cases that bear directly on the issues in question]. Finally, I would need to know how the legally correct answer would go over with the client politically; if I had not had any contact with the client directly, I would want to talk to other lawyers in the firm who have. If you put a gun to my head, though, and told me I had to answer on the spot, I would say that the client is taking a serious legal risk in doing what he proposes to do, and I would advise him against taking further action until we could furnish him with a more studied answer." This answer may not be totally satisfying, but it will answer the interviewer's "real" question of how you solve problems; note especially that you took into account not only the need for a correct legal analysis, but also the need to tailor the answer to the client's political situation. This usually will impress a lawyer-interviewer, whose primary job is to keep his clients happy and in compliance with the law, not necessarily to find legally correct answers that nobody can use.

Summary. Because this is such an important subject, I think it is useful to review some of the most important points about answering an interviewer's questions during a legal job interview:

--you must always look for the "hidden" question lurking beneath the "surface" question, and be sure to provide the information the interviewer is really looking for;

--preparation is everything; in an ideal situation there should be no question which you have not anticipated in advance;

--you must always tailor the answer to your interviewer's situation; your answers must always demonstrate a "fit" with the legal environment and culture of that particular employer, and must show the interviewer that deep down you are the same sort of person as he is;

--you never volunteer negative information about yourself;

--you never indicate that a question has surprised you or caught you unaware;

--you keep your answer short, concise and to the point;

--you remain silent after you have given your answer; if an uncomfortable silence ensues, you ask a follow up question or one of your prepared questions;

--you never relax or let your guard down, especially if the question is a seemingly harmless one about your outside interests;

--don't fudge an answer; if you don't know, try to buy time to find the right answer or (in the case of a technical legal question) tell the interviewer what you would do and what you would need to know in order to come up with an answer that works.

CHAPTER 8

A FINAL THOUGHT:
THE GOOD INTERVIEWER
NEVER STOPS INTERVIEWING

This book is about the legal job interview, but if there is one thing I would want every reader to take away from this book, it is that interviewing skills are part of your everyday life and work as a lawyer. When they talk about a lawyer "counseling" a client, what do they mean? What else if not an "interview", where the lawyer (interviewer) is trying either to persuade the client (candidate) that he should take or refrain from taking certain action because of the legal consequences involved, or to elicit information from that client that will help the lawyer find the legally correct solution? Perhaps this is why the clinical legal studies course in client handling, which is offered at just about every law school in the United States, is invariably called "Interviewing and Counseling."

Interviewing skills are not put on the shelf once one has received a job offer or otherwise passed beyond the stage of interviewing for a job. When dealing with a client or with his colleagues in everyday business situations, the lawyer is selling himself just as much as during a legal job interview, only more subtly so. The same techniques that are necessary to impress a lawyer-interviewer favorably are the same techniques necessary to win over a client or colleague who for various motives may have just as much reason to try to "screen you out" as a lawyer interviewer who must pick a winner out of a hatful of qualified candidates.

The good interviewer never stops interviewing; he hones and polishes his skills to a fine gloss, makes mental notes or written files of recurring interview situations, and forever seeks to come across in the light most favorable to himself, while focusing all of his concentration and energy on making the "other guy" open up, do all the talking, and maybe make a mistake or two.

There is a saying in Zen Buddhism that "you cannot pour water into a cup that is already full." What is meant is that you cannot learn anything, by reading something written by someone else or listening to what someone else has to say, when you are yourself talking or are focused on the ideas and thoughts randomly whirring through your head at the speed of light (the Zen Buddhists also say "the mind is like a drunken monkey"). One of the first lessons in any speed reading course is to stop verbalizing in your mind the words that you read on the printed page -- to let your eyes scan the words quickly without anything happening between your ears. Amazingly, you retain the information better this way than by reading each word and sounding it out in your head.

To truly absorb information from the outside world you must quiet yourself internally, literally "turn yourself off" like a light bulb, so that you can catch not only the words and pictures coming in from without, but also feel the rhythm and the music -- the tone of voice and body language of the person speaking, the context in which he places information -- that in the end may tell you more about the other person and what he is trying to tell you than the words themselves.

This process of "turning yourself off" and focusing the interview on the other person lies at the heart of successful legal job interviewing. I respectfully submit that it lies at the heart of the lawyer's life and work as well.

Good luck.

And remember:

You Already Have The Job

Warm, Friendly, Smile, Low Key

Calm, Confidence, Courage, Control

Say As Little As Possible

Don't Volunteer Any Negatives About Yourself

Don't Relax

ABOUT THE AUTHOR

Clifford R. Ennico practices corporate, commercial and business law with Kleban & Samor, P.C. in Southport, Connecticut, where he specializes in the legal and financial problems of the growing business.

Mr. Ennico received his B.A. degree in 1975 from Dartmouth College, and his J.D. degree in 1980 from Vanderbilt University School of Law, where he was Articles Editor of the *Vanderbilt Law Review* and law clerk to the late New York State Comptroller, Arthur Levitt Sr.

Mr. Ennico is the author and/or editor of several prominent legal publications, and is a frequent contributor to legal journals and small business magazines. He is Editor of *Corporate Practice Handbook*, the New York State Bar Association's legal guide for business lawyers, corporate executives and small business owners, and the author of *The Business Lawyer's Handbook*, a practical guide to the corporate lawyer's life and work which has established Mr. Ennico's reputation as a leading expert on legal career management.

Mr. Ennico frequently speaks to bar associations, college and law school students, business groups and civic organizations around the nation about legal developments affecting the business community, the legal problems of entrepreneurs and business owners, and managing the legal career. Information about Mr. Ennico's availability for speaking engagements can be obtained by writing Biennix Corporation, 2490 Black Rock Turnpike, Suite 407, Fairfield, Connecticut 06430-2404, Attention: Speaker's Bureau.

Mr. Ennico, who is admitted to practice in New York and Connecticut, is a Fellow of the American College of Investment Counsel and a member of the Connecticut Bar Association, the New York State Bar Association, and the Corporate Bar Association of Westchester and Fairfield Counties.